Praise
for
Bring Your Own Shark

Bring Your Own Shark is a refreshing and insightful take on the nuances of personal growth in a fast-changing world. Author Navinder Narang utilises compelling metaphors and relatable storytelling to highlight the fact that transformation begins with the challenges which we intentionally embrace. This remarkable book encourages readers to step out of their comfort zones, confront their internal barriers, and build momentum with purpose. It is a pragmatic, uplifting, and relevant treatise for professionals at every stage of their journeys. A fantastic guide for anyone seeking clarity, courage, and self-driven progress

—Vivek Atray Former IAS Officer, Author & Motivational TEDx Speaker

Navinder blends his military and corporate experiences into a brilliant allegory for growth in **BYOS**. Through powerful shark analogies, he captures how challenges shape leaders, turning adversity into strength. A must-read for anyone navigating business, career transitions, or personal reinvention in today's demanding world.

—Lt Gen CB Ponnappa (Retd), Former Adjutant General, Indian Army, HR & Veterans Affairs Strategist

This is such an absorbing work by Navinder Narang for anyone who is feeling a loss of mojo or direction. A highly educative leverage of the shark-world to the world of careers and life, this is easy to read and visually assimilative. A must-read for anyone who seeks to look within to move ahead. Nothing can be better than **BYOS**.

—Prabir Jha, Founder & CEO,
Prabir Jha People Advisory

Sailing solo around the world teaches you that growth comes from embracing the unknown, much like the lessons in **BYOS**. Navinder Narang brilliantly captures how challenges—like the sharks of the ocean—can push us beyond our limits and shape who we become. A compelling read for anyone navigating the rough waters of career and life.

—Abhilash Tomy, Solo Circumnavigator,
Former Naval Commander

BYOS offers powerful, thought-provoking ideas through relatable anecdotes and real-life stories that inspire transformation.

In this book, sharks serve as metaphors for challenges — and challenges are opportunities in disguise. A truly transformational toolkit for growth.

- Dr. Annurag Batra, Chairman & Editor in Chief -
BW Businessworld

BYOS holds up a mirror in front of the reader, and rather than making them pause and ponder, drives them into action. Simple, clear and impactful action. At different crossroads through our lives – personal and professional, we need to harness different strategies and strengths.

BYOS helps us quickly identify these strategies and how we can use them in that situation.

- Punit Sood, Independent Director,
ICICI Bank & NPCI

What resonated with me most was the central idea of **BYOS**—choosing challenges and embracing discomfort with intent, rather than waiting for life to throw them at us. It is a rare and empowering insight that, I believe, every teenager should be exposed to early in life. What a strong foundation this could build for resilience, courage, and purpose.

- Rajiv Vaishnav, Managing Partner, Cornerstone Ventures & General Partner, Quantum X Frontiers General Partner

I am intrigued by the powerful concept of embracing challenges as a catalyst for Growth. The way Navinder has drawn leadership lessons from different Shark Archetypes in **BYOS** makes the learning both engaging and actionable.

- Pawan Bhansali, Sr Executive Vice President,
Bajaj Housing Finance

BRING YOUR OWN SHARK

BRING YOUR OWN SHARK

Find and Embrace Your Unique Path to Growth

NAVINDER NARANG

NU VOICE PRESS

First published by NU VOICE PRESS 2026
An imprint of Hubhawks Pvt. Ltd
www.nuvoicepress.com

This is a work of non-fiction. Space and time have been rearranged to suit the convenience of the book. Except for public figures, hotels, and institution names, any resemblance to persons living or dead or the real events are purely coincidental.

ISBN: 978-81-993531-1-4
Typeset by Pooja Sharma
Published by Nu Voice Press

Disclaimer

The opinions, insights, and perspectives expressed in this book are solely those of the author and do not reflect the views or positions of any organisation, employer, or individual associated with the author, past or present. While this book draws inspiration from real-world scenarios, many of the stories, characters, and events have been fictionalised or modified for illustrative purposes. Any resemblance to actual persons or organisations, living or dead, is purely coincidental unless otherwise stated.

Mentions of real-world personalities and public figures are based on publicly available information and are used strictly for illustrative, educational, or inspirational purposes. These references do not imply any endorsement, partnership, or association with the author or publisher. The interpretations presented are entirely the author's own. This book is intended for informational and personal development purposes only, and the author and publisher shall not be held liable for any consequences arising from the use or interpretation of its contents.

Foreword

By Harish Mehta, Co-Founder of NASSCOM, Author of The Maverick Effect

We are moving into a future where change will not wait for readiness. And in that future, more than any tools or more skills that could prepare us, it is the ability to think clearly, to think independently, and to respond with courage when there is no playbook.

Bring Your Own Shark (BYOS) doesn't claim to offer answers. What it does offer is a nudge, and a bold one at that. It invites readers to reflect, to rethink their relationship with comfort, and to choose their own version of disruption before disruption chooses them.

When we worked to bring NASSCOM into being, we had no certainty that it would work. There was resistance and disbelief, especially within the system. I remember how the then Secretary of the Department of Electronics, Mr N. Vittal, had to be convinced of the Indian software industry's potential. What shifted his view was not just data, but the sight of competitors coming together, united in purpose. That unity brought credibility and clarity, eventually leading to policy. And that shared belief opened doors, even at global institutions like the World Bank, which began to see the Indian software industry through a new lens.

Looking back, we could take those risks because we had little to lose, but everything to imagine. And that freedom created space for courage, clarity, and collaboration. These same values are reflected throughout *BYOS*, not through grand institutional stories, but through deeply personal ones.

Each "shark" in this book represents a different form of growth tension through stories on urgency, ownership, adaptability, confrontation, and each story helps readers identify the kind of challenge they may need to invite into their own lives. The message is subtle but powerful: don't wait for the world to shape you. Shape yourself for the world that's coming.

The hidden chapter especially stood out to me as a nice surprise at the end. It reminded me that not all growth is forged over fire. Some of it takes root in stillness, empathy, and the quiet confidence of those who build others up. The future, as I see it, will need both energies: those who challenge and those who hold space.

BYOS doesn't aim to change industries. It aims to awaken individuals. And in doing that, it may help many people step into the future, not with fear, but with readiness.

And that, is timeless.

Harish Mehta

Foreword

By Bhawna Datta, Ultra-Marathoner & Spiritual Healer

There's something deeply transformative about choosing a path that most people would never imagine for themselves, whether it's running 100 kilometres or walking the inward journey of healing and awareness.

Bring Your Own Shark is not a book that asks you to change. It asks you to wake up to what's holding you back, to what lies dormant within, and to the truth that discomfort is often the doorway to alignment.

In my experience as a marathoner, the body doesn't evolve in comfort. It grows in those quiet, aching moments when your mind wants to give up, but your spirit says, "Just one more step." As a healer, I've seen that the same is true for the heart. Growth begins not when we avoid the pain—but when we learn to hold it, breathe through it, and let it teach us.

This book mirrors that philosophy beautifully. The shark, as used here, is not a threat but a teacher. Each chapter invites you to meet a different kind of energy: urgency, accountability, patience, empathy. And just like in life, you don't choose which energy shows up—you choose how ready you are to receive it.

What I love most about *BYOS* is that it doesn't glorify struggle. It honours intention. It reminds us that real power is not in braving the storm, but in learning to invite it—knowing that something in you is ready to rise.

If you're holding this book, trust me, it's not by chance. Somewhere, something in you is ready to swim with your shark. And that is where the journey begins.

Bhawna Datta

Preface

Every journey of transformation starts with a trigger: a moment, an idea, or a realisation that refuses to let go. For me, it was the timeless story of the Japanese fish tanks. A simple yet profound metaphor that revealed how growth is not just about ambition but also about introducing the right catalyst into your environment.

We all have those moments when progress slows down, motivation wanes, and success seems out of reach. While facing such moments becomes a *fait accompli*, the moot question is how we respond to them.

This book was born out of that question.

The next logical question for the readers would be: **Why sharks?** Well, sharks are the perfect metaphor for two reasons:

- Most of us become fearful of the challenges that confront us, much like we presume the sharks are to be feared. However, by examining these challenges more closely, we can discover strategies to overcome them, just like how sharks use their unique traits to dominate the food chain.

- Sharks are primal, relentless, and unapologetically focused. Each type of shark carries a distinct set of behaviours and survival strategies, offering unique lessons for navigating challenges in life and work.

There is one more perspective on sharks, which, if ignored, would be a disservice to these remarkable creatures. During my research on shark species and their behaviour, I was confronted with a deeply unsettling reality. The very apex predators that maintain the balance of marine ecosystems are being slaughtered at an alarming rate.

It was shocking to discover that over 100 million sharks are killed annually, the majority for their fins, which are stripped from their bodies in a cruel trade that leaves them to perish helplessly in the ocean. One haunting image that has stayed with me is on a remote beach in the Nicobar group of islands, where I stood as a mute spectator, watching two fishermen carry baskets overflowing with shark fins. It was a stark reminder of how little we question the destruction of what we fear.

I hope that, beyond its lessons on leadership and resilience, this book also helps dispel the myths and manufactured fear surrounding sharks, fuelled by movies like *Jaws*, *Deep Blue Sea*, and *47 Meters Down*. Sharks do not attack humans at will. They are not the villains of the sea; they are its protectors. Perhaps, by shifting our perspective, we can begin to respect and protect them as they deserve.

Many of the stories in the chapters are inspired by real-life moments that tested my resilience, decision-making, and adaptability. These narratives carry a semblance of my personal experiences, reflecting aspects of my real-life roles as:

- A High Altitude and Warfare School (HAWS) qualified combat skier
- A veteran with expertise in counter-insurgency and anti-terrorism operations, including a tenure in the tropical terrain of the Nicobar Islands
- A Facilities Manager who transitioned into becoming a Digital Transformation champion and sustainability professional
- A husband of an aneurysm survivor, witnessing firsthand the power of patience, determination, and recovery

Looking back, I realise that there have been pivotal moments in my life where the right decision could have accelerated my growth, while hesitation or error of judgement led to setbacks. From my early days at NDA Khadakwasla to my recent efforts to reinvent myself and stay relevant beyond the retirement age, every phase of my journey has been shaped by such defining moments.

At times, I had the clarity and courage to act decisively, making bold choices that propelled me forward. But in other instances, I failed to recognise fleeting opportunities, leading to delayed decisions that shaped my professional and personal journey in ways I only understood much later. These experiences, both wins and missteps, have given me a deep appreciation for the power of awareness, decisiveness, and adaptability.

With this book, my intent is to share these learnings in a way that is engaging, thought-provoking, and applicable. In today's world, where time is scarce and attention spans are fleeting, I have made a conscious effort to keep the stories precise and the lessons direct, focusing only on what truly matters.

I sincerely hope that this book not only engages you but also offers perspectives that help you navigate your own defining moments with clarity and conviction.

Insight from the Shark World

By Cristina Zenato, Professional Diver, Shark Behaviourist & Conservationist

"Sharks come in all shapes, sizes, and species; each has a unique way of navigating the ocean, their role, and their relationship within the vast web of nature. Understanding how they operate allows us to find a connection with our strengths and weaknesses."

"This book metaphorically invites us not to wait for a shark to enter the fish tank, but for us to become the shark—the reason why we act."

"An easy and fluid read with life examples comparable to our experiences, it teaches us to swim more efficiently, to select our goals, and to remain focused."

Author's Note

Cristina Zenato's work in the ocean's depths has always inspired awe and respect. Her relationship with sharks, apart from science and skill, is also rooted in trust, understanding, and presence. I am deeply honoured to have her words in this book. They remind us that sharks are not just symbols of fear or aggression but also guides to self-awareness, purpose, and flow.

Navinder Narang

Introduction

The Japanese Fish Tank Story: A Fresh Perspective

The Japanese have always had a deep love for fresh fish. But as fish populations near the coast dwindled, fishermen had to venture farther out to sea. The long journeys meant that by the time they returned, the fish were no longer fresh.

To solve this, they first installed freezers, which didn't work as frozen fish lacked the fresh taste. Then they tried live tanks, but with no predators, the fish became sluggish. The people could tell.

The final solution? **Introduce a shark into the tank**.

The fish, now alert and constantly moving, remained lively until they reached the shore. The Japanese finally had their fresh, lively fish.

At first glance, the shark seemed like the perfect motivator, pushing the fish into action. But here's the real question:

What happens when the shark is removed?

The Flaw in Fear-Driven Growth

Now imagine yourself as one of those fish. Your life is predictable. Comfortable. You slow down. Then, one day, someone throws a shark into your tank: a new boss, a crisis, a deadline. Suddenly, you're moving like never before, pushed by fear, urgency, and survival instincts.

Your energy is up. Your senses are sharp. You are fully alive.

But what happens when the shark is removed?

You go back to your old habits. Why? Because the energy wasn't yours; it was the shark's fear controlling you.

This is how most companies, schools, and families push growth.

They introduce pressure in the form of deadlines, grades, tests, and job threats.

They create fear, so people move faster.

They call it motivation, but it's really just survival mode.

And here's the truth: **Fear-driven growth is temporary**.

- It boosts action but kills creativity.
- It drives productivity but crushes long-term motivation.
- Just like the fish, the moment the external force disappears, you return to inertia.

So, what if there was another way?

What if you didn't need someone else's shark to push you?

What if you could "**Bring Your Own Shark**" (BYOS)?

The BYOS Mindset: Take Charge of Your Growth

This is where BYOS shifts the narrative.

Instead of relying on fear-driven pressure, BYOS invites you to introduce challenges that align with your personal goals and values.

This book is about:

✓ Identifying the right 'shark' for your tank, the one that pushes you forward, not out of fear, but out of inspiration, ambition, and purpose.

- ✓ Building self-motivation instead of waiting for someone else to push you.
- ✓ Choosing the challenges that drive your personal growth, rather than being forced into survival mode.

The Sharks in This Book: How the Chapters Are Grouped

Just like in the ocean, different sharks serve different roles. In BYOS, each shark represents a specific challenge that drives growth.

The shark chapters in this book are grouped in three parts, each focusing on a different stage of personal and professional development:

Part 1: Sharks That Spark Immediate Action - These sharks push you out of inertia and get you moving.

Part 2: Sharks That Build Long-Term Strength - These sharks teach consistency, patience, and resilience.

Part 3: Sharks That Master Complex Environments - These sharks help you navigate the uncertainty, conflict, and leadership challenges.

Each chapter introduces a fictional story that immerses you in the shark's lesson with a key insight, followed by reflections and 'shark exercises' ending with a real-world case study.

Not all sharks are aggressive. Some guide you with precision. Some challenge you subtly. Others push you into action. The key is to find the shark that fits your journey.

Don't wait for someone to push you. Bring your own shark.

You are still the fish in the tank. But this time:

- ◆ You aren't running away from fear; you are running toward growth.

- You aren't waiting for a boss, teacher, or crisis to push you; you create your own challenge.
- You aren't forced to react; you choose to act.

Here's how it works:

1. The chapters help you to identify your growth challenge.
2. You are able to choose the shark that fits that challenge.
3. The shark doesn't chase you; rather, it works with you. So, the fear element is removed.

As you take the quiz at the beginning of each part, you might realise that you resonate with more than one shark. That's perfectly normal. The sharks you identify with will often be shaped by the context of your current challenges, subconscious influences, and the situations playing out in your mind. Growth isn't about choosing just one; it's about understanding when to bring the right shark into your tank.

This Book's Promise to You

This book will not tell you to "just work harder" or "stay positive".

Instead, it will teach you how to grow on your terms.

Every person has a growth-related challenge. We have identified nine sharks whose natural traits address such challenges, and for each challenge, there is a specific shark chapter.

Here's what is expected of you:

- ✓ **Identify the shark that you need**: Recognise the trait that will push you forward.
- ✓ **Bring it into your tank**: Consciously embrace the challenge it represents

- ✓ **Embody the Shark response and evolve**: Internalise its strength and outgrow your limitations.

Don't wait for growth to come to you. Bring it.

And yes! Not all growth is about responding to challenges. Sometimes, transformation happens because of the right environment, one that nurtures confidence instead of forcing urgency. More on that later... let me not spill the beans too early.

So, are you ready to meet your 'shark'?

Let's dive into **Part 1** of your journey to discover the sharks that define 'action'.

Prelude

Have you ever flung a pebble like a frisbee and watched it create ripples and splashes on the surface of water that was so still? What did you think before you curved your forefinger to throw that pebble?

Go further back to when you were a child who had just learnt how to crawl. The moment you saw a few steps, what made you try and crawl up those steps?

There were other similar moments too, now that you started thinking, isn't it? The moment before you decided to choose your mainstream subjects, your first job, your life partner, and so on.

There is a moment before every great movement, a stillness so subtle that most of us miss it.

It is not ambition.

It is not fear.

It is **curiosity**.

Curiosity is the first ripple in the still water of our lives. It doesn't roar like a wave; it begins with a quiet question:

What if...?

Could I...?

Is there more?

Long before any shark is brought into the tank, curiosity stirs the water. It wakes something dormant: a restlessness, a pull toward the unknown. Sometimes, it shows up as the urge to try something new. Sometimes, it hides behind a question we're too shy to ask. And other times, it speaks in silence, when you find yourself looking at your own life and wondering, "Is this it?"

Every great shift begins there.

You've probably felt it.

The nudge to raise your hand in a meeting. The itch to apply for a role you're "not fully ready" for. The quiet thought that says, "There has to be another way to live and work."

I've felt it too, again and again. Looking back, almost every big turn in my life started with curiosity tapping me on the shoulder.

When I was still a student from a completely civilian background, the world of the armed forces felt distant and almost unreal, like something you saw in movies. My uncle would visit us in his olive greens, and the room changed: the posture, the stories, the energy. I remember thinking as a kid, "What is life like behind that uniform?"

That question stayed. So, when the opportunity came to appear for the SSB entrance examination for the NDA, logic could easily have said, "This isn't for you. You don't belong there." But curiosity was louder. I didn't go because I was sure I would get through. I went because I wanted to know. To see that world from the inside, not from the outside of the drawing room.

That's the thing about curiosity: it just refuses to let you stay where you are.

The same pattern repeated in training.

Those long runs, obstacle courses, punishing schedules: they weren't just tests of strength. For me, they were answers to a simple inner question:

"If so many before me have done this, why can't I?"

I was curious about my own limits. How far could the body go if the mind didn't give up first? The doubt was there, of course. But curiosity added a line after the doubt: "...Let's find out."

When I joined the infantry, curiosity took on a new shape. It was no longer just, "Can I do this?" It became, "What does it really mean to lead?"

Not in a textbook sense. But in the messy, unpredictable, everyday reality of people, terrain, and pressure. What does a leader look like when no one is watching? How do you earn trust, not just demand it? I wanted to experience that, and not just admire it in others.

Every patrol, every decision, every quiet conversation with my team was, in a way, an ongoing experiment in leadership. Curiosity kept asking, "What kind of leader do you want to become?" And more importantly, "What are you willing to change in yourself to get there?"

Years later, when the uniform had become a second skin and the army felt like home, curiosity came knocking again; this time with a much harder question:

What exists beyond this life you now know so well?

Can you be just as useful and fulfilled outside the comfort of ranks, structure, and a clear identity?

Leaving the army on premature retirement was not a decision made on the whims of emotions. Neither was it made because I had figured out my journey. It was because the question wouldn't go away. I was curious, almost stubbornly so, about the civilian world. About whether the values, discipline, and experience from service could be translated into success in a completely different arena.

On paper, it looked like a risk. Inside, it felt like following the same ripple that had taken me to the NDA gate years ago.

And then came the next wave of curiosity.

Digital transformation. ESG. Sustainability. New business models.

None of these came with a user manual for "former infantry officers". But the thought that kept surfacing was simple:

How far can we push the boundaries?

Once again, curiosity refused to let me stay in the shallow end. It pushed me into experimenting with new sectors, new skills, and new collaborations. Many things worked. Many things didn't. But every attempt added another layer to the answer to that first question: "Is there more?"

So, when I talk about curiosity in this book, I'm not speaking as a distant observer. I've watched it pull me into unfamiliar spaces, unimaginable roles and unknown oceans I didn't even know existed when I started.

Curiosity is the spark that summons the shark.

Without it, the ocean remains still. Without it, even the bravest fish will circle the same rock, mistaking the tank for the world. With it, the water itself seems to lean forward, as if inviting you to swim a little further.

Curiosity doesn't seek perfection. It seeks experience. It doesn't give you any guarantee that you'll win. It simply refuses to let you stay unchanged. It is the only force that can make us fall a little bit in love with uncertainty, and in that strange love, we find courage.

Curiosity turns fear into fascination.

It transforms hesitation into movement.

It creates that beautiful intersection where the question, "What if?" slowly becomes, "Why not?"

And here's the important part:

The very fact that you are even thinking about "bringing your own shark" (choosing your own challenge, instead of waiting for one to be thrown at you) means something has already shifted inside you. Your thoughts have crossed an invisible bridge from casual wondering to a real willingness to act.

Most people never notice that moment. They feel the nudge, they feel the discomfort, and then they drown it in busyness, distraction, or excuses. In other words, they stay at the edge of the water, making detailed plans about swimming without ever touching the ocean.

But that's not you.

If you've picked up this book, it's probably because some part of you is already curious:

- Curious about your own potential.
- Curious about a different way of growing.
- Curious about what might happen if, for once, you chose your own challenge instead of waiting for life to choose it for you.

So, before you bring your shark into the tank, pause for a moment.

Ask yourself:

- What am I genuinely curious about right now?
- What keeps tugging at my mind when the world falls quiet?
- What do I secretly want to try, even if I'm not ready to admit it to others yet?

That is where your journey begins—not with a big, dramatic decision, but with a small, honest question that refuses to go away.

Because every ocean starts with a single drop.

And every shark story starts with a single ripple: **the ripple of curiosity.**

Contents

Part 1: Thriving in Action

Action separates the dreamers from the doers. The sharks in the first three chapters of this book will teach you how to thrive in moments of high intensity where speed, focus, and courage shape your path to success.

Discover Your Shark Quiz - 1

The **Mako Shark**, the **Hammerhead Shark**, and the **Bull Shark** together symbolise dynamic action in different forms. This quiz will help you identify if you need any of them in your tank.

Answer the questions below with Yes or No:

1. **Do you find yourself overthinking** tasks instead of completing them?
2. **Do you struggle with maintaining focus** on your goals?
3. **Are you comfortable with facing conflict** head-on?

Check if you find your shark(s) below:

- **Yes to Question 1**: You need the **Mako Shark**, which will teach you to act decisively and overcome hesitation (**Speed**).
- **Yes to Question 2**: You need the **Hammerhead Shark**, which will help you maintain discipline and eliminate distractions (**Focus**).
- **No to Question 3**: Bring the **Bull Shark**, it will teach you to face adversity head-on with boldness and determination (**Courage and Grit**).

Come, let's get acquainted with each of these sharks and the wonderful change they can bring to the tank.

Chapter 1:
The Mako Shark – Speed & Urgency

Meet the Mako Shark

Scientific Name: *Isurus oxyrinchus*

Habitat: Open oceans, known for long-distance migrations.

Behaviour: Fast, agile, and relentless predators, capable of reaching speeds up to 74 km/h.

Unique Trait: Known for their incredible bursts of speed and sharp reflexes.

A creature built for speed, the Mako Shark dominates the open waters with unmatched agility and focus.

Story: "The Seconds that Changed Everything for Emma"

1. The High Adrenalin Moment Before the Race: A Career at a Crossroads

Emma stood at the starting gate of the **Hahnenkamm Downhill Finals** in Kitzbühel, Austria, declared the most dangerous ski race in the world.

A gust of icy wind rushed up the slopes, biting through her suit, but Emma barely noticed. Her focus was locked on the 3,300 metre course before her, with a near-vertical drop at sections and pure ice on others, the kind of terrain that separated the fearless from the cautious.

Competitors on this course hurtle down at up to 140 km/h. Every turn demands perfect precision. Every single mistake can result in crashes that have sidelined even the best skiers for an entire season.

Emma had raced on many brutal slopes before this and had her share of learnings:

- In Lake Louise, Canada, she crashed out in a World Cup event after misjudging a turn.
- In Cortina d'Ampezzo, Italy, she played it safe on a tricky section and finished outside the podium.
- In the Beijing Winter Olympics, hesitation cost her a medal, placing her in a forgettable fourth place.

That last one stung the most.

The media had all but written her off after Beijing.

"Maybe she doesn't have the killer instinct."

"She's good, but she doesn't take risks."

Emma had spent months wrestling with that failure. She told herself that playing it safe had been the right move. But deep down, she knew the truth.

She hadn't lost because she was slower.

She had lost because she **hesitated**.

Now, standing at the top of the Hahnenkamm, she promised herself:

Not today. Not this time.

This was the race that could change everything.

2. The Descent: Speed or Safety?

Five seconds.

Emma adjusted her goggles, blocking out everything except the course ahead.

Four seconds.

The red-marked shortcut flashed in her mind. This was an uncharted territory.

Three seconds.

Her coach's words: "Play it safe, and you'll finish top five. Risk it, and you might take gold."

Two seconds.

Her career had been defined by caution. Today, she would own the moment.

One second.

The buzzer sounded.

She pushed off, her skis slicing into the ice, her body absorbing the first bone-rattling impact as she accelerated past 110 km/h (68 mph).

The first minute was all muscle memory, making fast, aggressive and powerful turns. The slope dropped beneath her, and she leaned into the descent, feeling her speed build like a force of nature.

Then she reached the turning point.

Ahead was a sweeping curve, which was the safe route where she'd keep control but likely finish fourth again.

To the right, barely visible through the snow spray, was the shortcut, a near-vertical drop leading to an ice chute.

No one had ever taken it in competition.

One second to decide.

"The Mako Shark doesn't hesitate. It launches forward at breathtaking speed, slicing through the water with precision."

For Emma, speed wasn't just about moving fast. It was about having the confidence to make a decision and act on it before the opportunity passed.

3. The Leap of Faith: Breaking the Mould

She went for it.

Emma shifted her weight, cutting sharply right toward the chute.

The crowd gasped as she launched off the drop-off, with her skis slicing through the air and the mountain falling away beneath her.

For a split second, she was airborne. Weightless. Vulnerable.

The icy slope rushed toward her too fast.

She landed hard, with her edges barely gripping the ice.

Hold it. Hold it.

Her right ski wobbled.

She dug in, clenching every muscle to stabilise.

Milliseconds saved.

She shot down the chute like a bullet, merging back onto the main track, now ahead of the leader's pace.

She had done what no one dared to do.

Thirty seconds to go.

4. The Finish Line: Did It Pay Off?

Emma attacked the final stretch, her body screaming, but her mind focused.

The finish line approached.

She had no idea if she was ahead or behind.

She threw herself forward, crossing the line.

The world blurred. Then, the scoreboard flashed:

"First Place – New Course Record."

The crowd erupted. Emma collapsed onto the snow, gasping for breath.

She had done it!

She had raced like the Mako Shark. No hesitation, no fear, boldly choosing **speed over safety.**

5. A Career Transformed: The Risk That Changed Everything

That one second of courage changed everything for Emma.

- She became a ski legend overnight.
- Brands lined up to sponsor her.

- Journalists called it "the most daring move in skiing history."
- Her name became synonymous with fearless decision-making.

One moment, one choice led to a completely different trajectory.

And she had almost hesitated.

Emma realised then: *You don't get extra seconds to think. You take the shot, or you don't.*

The Mako Shark doesn't pause. It moves: **fast and fearless**.

Mako Shark Insight: The Sprint Strategy

✓ Act swiftly, decide confidently, and seize opportunities before they disappear.

✓ Don't let hesitation be the reason you miss your moment.

Procrastination still lingers in many moments of life, moments we must recognise and overcome.

Take a moment and look at your unfinished tasks:

- The draft presentation you're still tweaking.
- The email you've written but have not sent.
- The pitch idea that's sitting in your notebook.

Ask yourself:

What are you waiting for?

Which task are you overthinking?

Where are you choosing 'polished' over 'done'?

Mako Shark Exercise: Helping You Embrace Speed and Urgency

Do This Right Away: Choose one small decision or task you have been delaying. Complete it within the next hour, focusing on momentum over perfection.

Do This Later Today: Reflect on how taking action, even if imperfect, shifted your mindset or progress.

Real-World Example: How Jeff Bezos Displayed Mental Speed under Pressure

1. The Slow Tide

Jeff Bezos was always a brilliant strategist, but in his early years, he was following a traditional path in finance. After graduating from Princeton, he worked on Wall Street, excelling in hedge funds and technology investments.

While he had a comfortable career and financial security, he felt that something was missing. There was no sense of urgency to create something transformative. He had many innovative ideas, but he found himself still tied to the corporate world's slow, cautious and calculated approach.

He was successful, but he wasn't moving at the speed of innovation.

2. Spotting the Wave and Riding It

The defining moment came in 1994 when Bezos stumbled upon a report predicting explosive growth in internet usage.

- ✓ **The Projection**: Internet usage was growing at 2,300% per year, which was an unheard-of acceleration.
- ✓ **The Realisation**: If he didn't act now, he would miss the opportunity of a lifetime.

✓ **The Risk**: He was working at D.E. Shaw, a prestigious investment firm, and had a stable career ahead.

Bezos had two choices:

- Stay comfortable in his high-paying finance job.
- Move fast and take a massive risk on an unproven industry.

At that moment, the Mako Shark mentality kicked in. He couldn't wait for the 'perfect moment'. The internet was happening now, and if he didn't move at the speed of change, someone else would.

So, he quit his job and started **Amazon** out of his garage, betting everything on an idea that no one else had fully understood yet.

This was the moment Bezos stopped analysing the opportunity and started acting on it.

3. How Bezos Responded: Adapting Fast

Even after founding Amazon, many doubted him.

Investors called it a foolish gamble.

The media questioned whether people would buy books online.

Competitors like Barnes & Noble dismissed Amazon as a niche player.

But Bezos refused to slow down. Instead, he accelerated.

✓ **Speed Over Perfection**: Bezos prioritised fast execution over flawless plans. Instead of waiting for the perfect website, he launched quickly and improved it as he went.

✓ **The 'Two-Pizza Rule'**: He created Amazon's fast decision-making culture, ensuring no meeting was so big that two pizzas couldn't feed the entire team. Small, agile teams meant rapid decision-making.

✓ **Relentless Scaling**: Within four years, Amazon expanded from books to music, electronics, and consumer goods, outpacing traditional retailers.

Every decision he made aligned with the Mako Shark principle:

"Act fast. Adapt faster. Never hesitate."

By 1999, Amazon was no longer just an online bookstore. It was an e-commerce empire.

4. There's More to the Amazon Story

Bezos fully embodied the Mako Shark when Amazon faced its first real crisis: the dot-com crash of 2000.

The Crash: The stock plummeted by over 90%, wiping out billions in value.

Bezos' Response: Instead of slowing down, he pushed Amazon to move even faster, cutting inefficiencies, streamlining logistics, and expanding aggressively when others pulled back.

The Long-Term Payoff:

✓ By 2003, Amazon rebounded stronger than ever.

✓ By 2010, Amazon Web Services (AWS) had revolutionised cloud computing.

✓ By 2020, Bezos became the richest person in the world because he moved faster than his competitors.

Bezos' greatest strength wasn't just vision; it was his ability to act faster than hesitation, faster than fear, and faster than the market itself.

Go For It!

"Don't wait for the perfect moment. Bring the Mako Shark into your tank. Start moving."

Over to the Next Wave

Speed gives you an edge, but without focus, it can scatter your energy in too many directions. Now that you've learned to act with urgency, it's time to sharpen your clarity, just like the **Hammerhead Shark.**

Chapter 2: The Hammerhead Shark – Focus & Clarity

Meet the Hammerhead Shark

Scientific Name: *Sphyrnidae*

Habitat: Warm coastal waters and continental shelves.

Behaviour: Known for their wide field of vision and sharp observational skills.

Unique Trait: Their unique head shape enables panoramic vision for unparalleled focus.

With sharp focus and clarity, the Hammerhead Shark navigates chaos with precision.

Story: "The Art of Seeing Through Chaos"

1. The Rise of Chaos

Marina Bay, Singapore, is a stunning blend of modern architecture, vibrant city energy and waterfront elegance. The shimmering waters and the city's futuristic design symbolise ambition, movement and innovation.

The panoramic view of the bay glimmered through the floor-to-ceiling windows of the twenty-fifth-floor office. Inside, Zayden stared at his laptop, where six browser tabs blinked like nagging neon signs.

His phone buzzed incessantly, his inbox overflowed, and a sticky note on his monitor demanded attention:

"*Investor Presentation: Friday – Non-negotiable!*"

"Zayden, are we ready for Friday's demo?" Lucas, his manager, asked from outside the glass cubicle.

"Almost there," Zayden replied, masking his inner chaos. Inside, his brain felt like a browser with fifty open tabs, each one slowing down the system.

Just then, Elise Tan, the team's sharp-witted senior analyst, walked past his desk.

"You look like you're drowning in data," she said, smirking.

Elise Tan had a reputation for cutting through complexity with precision. She had once helped Zayden restructure an entire project plan in a single afternoon.

"Not drowning. Just navigating a storm," Zayden chuckled, but knew she had a point. **Focus was his missing piece**.

2. The Spiral of Distraction

The Friday demo was supposed to be Zayden's moment to shine, showcasing Ridge Capital's cutting-edge analytics tool to key investors.

But distractions hit like waves, leaving him adrift:

- HR escalated a minor interpersonal conflict in the team.
- A supplier email flagged an overdue compliance certificate.
- A bug in the demo code raised alarms.

By 11:30 PM Wednesday, Zayden was staring at his incomplete demo deck.

"Clarity creates momentum. Without it, we're just spinning wheels." Lucas's words echoed in his head.

Zayden Lim wasn't just another corporate executive; he was a rising star.

- At Harvard Business School, his leadership and determination made him stand out.
- Graduating Summa Cum Laude, Zayden chose Singapore over Wall Street, joining Ridge Capital.
- He had climbed the ranks in just three years, starting as an Analyst, going on to become a Senior Analyst and now a Junior VP.

His corner office overlooked Marina Bay Sands, a testament to his ambition.

But the higher he climbed, the thinner the air became. His inbox had become a battlefield, his sleep came in two-hour shifts, and cracks were starting to form beneath his polished exterior.

At thirty-one, Zayden was burning out.

His career had begun with ambition etched into every decision.

But clarity, the sharp focus that distinguishes leaders, was something he would need to cultivate amidst chaos.

3. Enter the Hammerhead Shark

At midnight, Zayden leaned back in his chair, eyes locked on his chaotic whiteboard, which looked like a patchwork of arrows, sticky notes and diagrams.

Zayden sighed and gazed out at Marina Bay, serene and endless under the midnight sky.

In his mind, he imagined a **Hammerhead Shark** gliding through the vast blue, eyes set wide apart, seeing the full picture but always locking onto its prey with **unwavering clarity**.

"Stop chasing everything, Zayden. Focus on the one thing that matters."

He grabbed a fresh sticky note and scribbled: "Deliver a flawless investor demo on Friday."

Zayden erased half the tasks from his to-do list, closed unnecessary tabs, and sent his team one clear message: "Focus Mode Activated. No distractions until the demo's done."

For the first time that week, Zayden felt his mind sharpen, like the wide-eyed Hammerhead scanning the ocean for its target.

The next morning, Zayden marked himself "Out of Office", muted all unnecessary notifications and dedicated his focus to refining the presentation.

✓ Calls to data analysts brought in additional insights.

✓ His slides were streamlined to convey a crystal-clear message.

✓ He even scheduled short breaks to regain composure.

By Thursday night, the deck was complete.

Zayden glanced at his final slide, took a deep breath, and called it a night.

4. The Investor Meeting

The conference room buzzed with quiet energy.

Zayden walked in, greeted by six investors seated around a polished glass table. A large screen displayed the title of his presentation:

"*Vision 2025: Scaling GreenTech beyond Boundaries.*"

He began with confidence, outlining his strategy:

✓ Market potential

✓ Competitive edge

✓ Execution roadmap

✓ Financial projections

The slides were crisp, the data compelling, and the investors leaned in with interest.

Just as the meeting seemed to flow smoothly, Mr Patel, one of the senior investors, raised a hand.

5. The Tough Question

"Zayden," Mr Patel began, his tone probing, "your strategy is impressive. But let's address the elephant in the room. What's your backup plan if your AI technology doesn't scale as intended? And how do you defend against competitors leapfrogging you?"

The room fell silent, the question hanging heavily in the air.

Zayden paused for a moment, then spoke with calm confidence:

"Thank you for asking that, Mr Patel. These are critical points, and we've built safeguards into both areas."

- **Scalability?** "Our AI has undergone stress testing to handle three times the anticipated load."

- **Competition?** "We've invested 30% of our revenue back into R&D, securing multiple patents to safeguard our IP."

Zayden leaned slightly forward, meeting Mr Patel's gaze.

"The truth is, risks will always exist. What differentiates us is our ability to anticipate, adapt, and execute with clarity. These are the qualities that guide every decision we make."

6. Clarity in Action: The Turning Point and Beyond

Mr Patel nodded, a faint smile breaking his stern demeanour.

"That's the kind of clarity we look for in a leader."

The room's energy shifted.

As the meeting concluded, Zayden stood by the window, allowing a quiet pride to wash over him.

He had navigated the challenge with precision, just like the **Hammerhead Shark**: sharp, focused, and fearless in the face of complexity.

Later that evening, as congratulatory messages buzzed on his phone, Elise Tan walked in with two coffees.

"Cheers to the Sharpshooter, Zayden. That's your new nickname."

Zayden laughed a rare, unguarded laugh.

Focus isn't about doing more. It's about choosing the one thing that matters and hitting it with everything you've got.

Over the next few weeks, Zayden's clarity became his defining trait. Meetings sharpened. Priorities crystallised. His team worked with renewed purpose. For the first time in months, Zayden felt everything appearing sharp and crystal clear.

Hammerhead Shark Lesson: Locked Vision

- ✓ Focus isn't about doing everything. It's about doing what matters most, with unwavering clarity.
- ✓ Clarity cuts through chaos.

Zayden's clarity didn't come from avoiding decisions. It came from prioritising them. Now, it's time to sharpen your focus.

- Where are you spreading yourself thin?
- Which tasks drain your energy without results?
- What would happen if you focused on just three critical tasks daily?

Hammerhead Shark Exercise: This Will Sharpen Your Focus and Clarity

Think of a long-cherished goal that is eluding you.

Do This Right Away: List three priorities that align with your goal. Also, eliminate one distraction or a low-priority task that is occupying your mind.

Do This When You Move Closer towards Your Goal: Reflect on how narrowing your focus improved your ability to address the task effectively.

Real-World Example: Staying Laser-Focused on the Goal

1. Stephen Hawking's Untapped Potential

Stephen Hawking was a highly intelligent and curious student, but his early academic career was not extraordinary. Despite his immense intellectual capabilities, his focus was scattered rather than channelled effectively.

In his early years, Hawking had a brilliant but undisciplined mind:

- ✓ As a child, he displayed deep curiosity about the universe but was often seen as a mediocre student.
- ✓ He had a rebellious streak, preferring to engage in self-directed learning. He had a deep love for science and mathematics, but lacked structured focus.
- ✓ His classmates nicknamed him "Einstein" because of his obvious brilliance, despite his seemingly careless academic performance.
- ✓ His time at Oxford University was marked by enthusiasm but not rigour. His problem-solving skills aided him during the exams.

Stephen Hawking had immense intellectual potential, but it was scattered rather than focused.

2. When Realisation Struck (The BYOS Moment)

In 1963, everything changed when Hawking was diagnosed with ALS (Lou Gehrig's disease) at just twenty-one years old.

Doctors gave him two years to live. His body would gradually lose the ability to move, but his mind would remain sharp.

He faced a stark choice: either surrender to his illness or find a way to make the most of his time.

Hawking realised he needed to eliminate all distractions and dedicate himself entirely to theoretical physics.

3. Hawking's Focused Response

Instead of giving up, Hawking cultivated an extraordinary ability to concentrate.

- ✓ He ignored the noise, blocked out unimportant distractions, and channelled all his mental energy into doing groundbreaking research.
- ✓ He refined his PhD thesis on black holes at Cambridge, despite his deteriorating health.

✓ Even as his body weakened, his mind grew sharper and more disciplined.

His work led to the **Hawking Radiation Theory**, one of the most profound contributions to modern physics.

4. Hawking's Transformation

Stephen Hawking embodied the **Hammerhead Shark's** ability to cut through complexity with absolute focus.

- In 1988, he published *A Brief History of Time*, making complex scientific ideas accessible to millions.
- His sharp focus on black holes and cosmology revolutionised astrophysics.
- Even when he lost the ability to speak, he continued his research using a speech-generating device.

Hawking's greatest strength was not his body, but his ability to direct his mind with precision.

Your Turn Now!

"Focus isn't about working harder. It's about working smarter. Bring the Hammerhead Shark into your tank. See everything, but act on what matters."

What Comes Next?

Clarity is powerful, but sometimes, the road ahead is tough. What happens when you face resistance, when your focus is challenged?

That's where courage comes in. Get ready to channel the fearless strength of the **Bull Shark**.

Chapter 3:
The Bull Shark – Courage and Grit

Meet the Bull Shark

Scientific Name: *Carcharhinus leucas*

Habitat: Thriving in both saltwater and freshwater, Bull Sharks are uniquely adaptable.

Behaviour: They face challenging environments head-on, using boldness and grit to dominate.

Unique Trait: Unyielding courage and the ability to adapt under any circumstances.

When the tides change, the Bull Shark powers through without hesitation.

Story: "When the Going Gets Tough"

1. Mumbai Marathon: 7:10 AM

The early morning sun had cast long shadows across Marine Drive, its golden glow bouncing off the Arabian Sea. A light breeze mixed with the scent of salt and the sweat of thousands of runners who pounded the barricaded road in the **Mumbai Marathon**, their breathing rhythmic, their steps synchronised.

Rohan Saxena felt the sting of exhaustion creeping into his legs.

Thirty-five kilometres done. Seven more to go.

He had started strong, with a steady pace, and his breathing was controlled. But now, his body was rebelling. The burn in his calves, the tightness in his chest, the dryness in his throat, they all whispered the same thing: Stop. Walk. Give up.

Runners ahead of him had started slowing down, some pausing to stretch, others stopping altogether. He knew this was the breaking point. His body was signalling that it had reached its limit.

But Rohan had learned that limits were meant to be pushed.

As his legs continued moving forward, his mind flashed back to another endurance test. One that had taken place just a week ago.

2. Bandra Kurla Complex (BKC), Mumbai: One Week Earlier

The morning rush at BKC was relentless. The financial hub of Mumbai pulsed with energy as regular Ola and Uber cabs weaved through luxury sedans, their honks blending into the hurried footsteps of thousands of professionals. Glass-walled corporate towers reflected the sun's morning glare, while coffee chains bustled with early meetings.

Stepping inside the boardroom at Rio Capital's twenty-eighth-floor headquarters, Rohan was about to fight a different kind of race. For the past year, Rohan has led the transformation of Rio's facilities management, introducing a state-of-the-art Building Management System (BMS) powered by AI and IoT. It was much more than a system upgrade. For users, and especially for Arjun Mehta, a junior manager in the facilities team, it was a cultural shift.

But not everyone had been on board.

The conference room doors opened, and Vikram Sethi, the firm's CFO, walked in with a document in hand. His expression was unreadable. But Rohan knew exactly what was coming. Vikram's voice was measured, yet firm:

"This system has been a massive expenditure. I don't see the returns you promised, Rohan. It's time we reconsider manual operations."

Rohan felt a surge of frustration.

The BMS was his brainchild. For the past year, he had worked tirelessly to create AI-driven facility automation, making the Titan office one of the most advanced workplaces in Mumbai.

- ✓ Energy consumption dropped by 18%.
- ✓ Operational efficiency improved by 23%.
- ✓ Employee complaints on workspace conditions reduced by 40%.

Yet, Vikram's priority lay in short-term cost reductions.

3. Back to the Marathon: The Breaking Point

Rohan's breath was now shallow, his body screaming at him to stop.

Just like in the boardroom, this was the moment of truth.

"This is where most people slow down. The real race begins now."

He wasn't running against the other competitors anymore. He was running against himself.

Just like that day in the boardroom, when backing down wasn't an option.

4. Enter the Bull Shark

*The **Bull Shark** is one of the only sharks that can survive in rivers and oceans, adjusting effortlessly between two worlds.*

For Rohan, grit wasn't just about endurance. It was about adapting to different challenges, whether in business or on the marathon trail. He realised that if things have to change, he will have to do something. Confrontation isn't the enemy. Avoidance is.

Rohan leaned forward, his eyes locked onto Vikram.

"The numbers don't tell the whole story, Vikram."

His voice was steady, but his pulse raced. He had to make them see beyond the spreadsheets. A thought occurred to him: "When pressure mounts, don't retreat; instead, lean into it."

This wasn't just about cost savings. This was about the future.

"Rio is competing with firms that have already embraced smart technology. If we slow down now, we will be left behind. The employees have experienced the difference, and productivity is at an all-time high. Rolling back this system would be a mistake."

Vikram's lips pressed into a thin line. A standoff. And then, an unexpected voice cut through the tension.

"Rohan is right."

Everyone turned toward the speaker. It was Arjun Mehta.

5. The Bull Shark Creates a Ripple

Arjun was usually quiet in these meetings. But today, something in Rohan's conviction had inspired him.

"I ran an additional analysis this morning," Arjun continued, his voice gaining confidence. "I've identified a small glitch that, if corrected, will improve the system's efficiency by another 5%. It makes the numbers even more favourable."

Rohan nodded. This was what leadership was about.

Not just winning your battles, but inspiring others to take ownership.

Arjun's input added the numbers to what Rohan was trying to put across so passionately.

6. Marathon: The Final Stretch

The final kilometre. Rohan's legs felt like lead, his vision blurred, but he kept moving. The crowd cheered him.

"I don't need to win this race. I just need to finish it strong."

As he neared the finish line, the thought struck him:

"It's never about whether you feel like pushing forward. It's about whether you do it anyway."

7. BKC: One Week Later

Vikram hadn't changed his stance overnight. But with the data from Arjun's analysis, the leadership team saw promise in the project and voted in favour of keeping the BMS system intact.

Rohan had won the battle, just like he had won the battle with himself in the Marathon.

Because **Bull Sharks** don't slow down when it gets hard; *they push through, adapting, fighting, and owning their space.*

Bull Shark Lesson: Bold Entry

✓ Courage is a muscle. Train it.

✓ If you won't confront it, you can't control it.

Next time you're faced with a moment where your mind says stop, ask yourself: Am I a Bull Shark, or am I waiting for permission?

Give a thought: Are you waiting for the "right moment," or will you create it?

Bull Shark Exercise: An Opportunity to Cultivate Courage and Grit

Do This Today: Think of a current challenge you have always hesitated to address. Take one bold step today to face the challenge, such as initiating a difficult conversation or tackling a daunting task.

Do This When You See Results Appearing: Reflect on how embracing courage affected your confidence or progress.

Real-World Example: Malala Yousafzai's Fearless Resilience Against All Odds

1. Resigned to her Fate?

Malala Yousafzai grew up in Mingora, Pakistan, in a household that valued education deeply.

Her father, Ziauddin Yousafzai, was a teacher and activist, running a local girls' school.

Malala loved learning, excelling in her studies, and dreaming of a future where all girls could access education.

However, in 2007, the Taliban took control of the Swat Valley, banning girls from attending school.

Malala's world shifted from hope to fear. But at this stage, she was just another girl watching her rights being taken away.

2. The BYOS Moment: Malala Confronts Injustice

In 2009, when Malala was just eleven years old, the Taliban forced hundreds of schools to shut down.

Instead of staying silent, Malala began writing an anonymous blog for BBC Urdu under the pen name "Gul Makai", describing life under Taliban rule.

Her words were fearless, detailing how oppression was crushing the future of young girls.

Her secret identity didn't last long. The world began to take notice.

Malala could have stayed silent, but she chose to confront danger head-on, just like the **Bull Shark**, which thrives in tough, unpredictable environments.

3. Malala only Knew One Way: Forward!

As Malala's voice grew louder, so did the threats against her life.

By 2011, she received Pakistan's National Youth Peace Prize, gaining international recognition. But her activism made her a target. The Taliban issued a death threat against her.

Instead of backing down, Malala continued her advocacy, refusing to let fear silence her.

4. Malala's Relentless Pursuit of Purpose

In 2012, Malala's courage was put to the ultimate test. While riding a school bus, a Taliban gunman shot her in the head at point-blank range.

The world held its breath as Malala fought for her life, undergoing multiple surgeries in Pakistan and later in the UK.

Instead of giving in to anger or fear, Malala became even more determined.

- ✓ **2013**: Co-founded the Malala Fund and delivered a speech at the United Nations advocating for girls' education.
- ✓ **2014**: Became the youngest-ever Nobel Peace Prize laureate at age seventeen.
- ✓ **2020**: Graduated from Oxford University with a degree in Philosophy, Politics and Economics.

Malala is today a global symbol of resilience, courage and change who is inspiring millions through her advocacy for girls' education, gender equality, and refugee rights.

True courage isn't just about surviving adversity. It's about using that pain to fuel a greater purpose. Malala did the same.

Time for You to go Full Throttle!

"Be the Bull Shark. Face your challenges boldly, choose to move forward with grit, and thrive in every aspect of your life, no matter what the odds are."

The Next Part: From Strength to Strategy

You have now discovered the sharks that create dynamism for action in the face of challenges. But leadership isn't just about fighting battles. It's about taking ownership, pacing yourself for long-term success, and adapting when challenges shift.

Now, in **Part 2** of this book, we move from raw courage to the mindset of sustained leadership. The next set of sharks—**Blacktip**, **Whale**, and **Tiger**—will show you how.

But, There's Another Perspective Too...

Standing your ground takes courage, but what if strength also lies in knowing when to step back, listen, and build trust? Some challenges aren't about force; they're about connection. Intrigued? Hold on to it, we'll come to that soon... I cannot reveal much at this stage.

Part 2: Adaptability in the Unknown

In the face of unpredictability, adaptability is key.

The sharks in the next three chapters will show you how **patience, accountability and flexibility** can help you master the unknown.

Discover Your Shark Quiz - 2

Identify whether you need the **Blacktip Shark**, the **Whale Shark**, or the **Tiger Shark**.

Answer the questions below with Yes or No:

1. **Do you struggle with taking ownership of your tasks?**
2. **Do you pursue your long-term goals with patience?**
3. **Do you despise sudden changes?**

Check the answers to find your shark(s) below:

- **Yes to Question 1**: Bring the **Blacktip Shark**: It will teach you to take ownership of your role and lead by example (**Accountability**).
- **No to Question 2**: Get the **Whale Shark**: It will make you embrace persistence and big-picture thinking (**Patience**).
- **Yes to Question 3**: Swim with the **Tiger Shark**: It will show you how to thrive in uncertainty and respond flexibly to change (**Adaptability**).

Chapter 4:
The Blacktip Shark – Ownership & Accountability

Meet the Blacktip Shark

Scientific Name: *Carcharhinus limbatus*

Habitat: Shallow coastal waters and coral reefs.

Behaviour: Agile and fast swimmers, frequently leaping out of the water.

Unique Trait: Known for their precision, control and quick decision-making.

An agile predator, the Blacktip Shark moves with precision and bold ownership of its environment.

Story: "Daniel's Defining Moment"

1. The Turning Point

The glass façade of the high-rise tower reflected the golden hues of the evening sun. Inside, the **forty-second-floor office of Al Manar Tech Ventures** buzzed with nervous energy. Floor-to-ceiling windows offered a panoramic view of Downtown Dubai, with the Burj Khalifa piercing the skyline in the distance.

At a central conference table, glowing laptop screens flickered with last-minute checks. A massive digital display showed three time zones—New York, London, and Dubai—signalling the global significance of the upcoming investor demo.

Then, chaos struck.

A key backend technology vendor had just backed out, leaving crucial integrations incomplete. Investors from three countries were flying in for the big reveal in a week. A failure could cripple the start-up's future.

All eyes turned to Daniel Carter, the Head of Product Development.

In the dimly lit war room, the CEO, Marcus Laine, sat forward, his jaw clenched.

"Daniel, can we still make this happen?"

Daniel's mind raced.

"If I don't step up now, who will? This isn't about avoiding risk. This is leading through uncertainty."

Instead of panicking, he started listing immediate options.

"Give me the night," he said. "I'll find a way."

Daniel didn't just take responsibility for solving the problem. He became the beacon of hope for his team.

2. The Crisis Deepens

As emails flew and phone calls stacked up, Daniel worked methodically, scanning for leverage points.

By dawn, he had found a small, agile AI development firm in Estonia that could step in.

But there was a catch.

The team required an immediate advance payment to start.

Daniel called Marcus.

"There's a way! We need to do real-time integration with no margin for error. But I need immediate approval for an advance payment."

Marcus sighed. "Daniel, the funds are locked in. You'll have to figure something else out."

The weight of the moment settled on Daniel's shoulders. He realised that ownership isn't just about taking responsibility when things go right; it's about making tough calls when the risks are real.

This was his call.

3. Enter the Blacktip Shark

Blacktip Sharks *don't hesitate. Their sharp movements and sudden bursts of speed ensure they strike at the right moment.*

Daniel realised that true ownership wasn't about waiting, but about taking action the moment it mattered. He made a bold choice: he used his personal savings for the initial advance payment, a decision rooted in his belief that decisive action is the foundation of ownership.

For forty-eight hours straight, he coordinated with the Estonian team while keeping his Dubai-based developers focused.

By the time the team reconvened in their Marina Plaza co-working space, Daniel looked exhausted but resolute.

"The integration is in. We're ready to run the first test demo."

The CTO, Mei Ling, placed a hand on his shoulder.

"You carried us through the storm, Daniel. That's what leadership looks like."

One developer raised a coffee cup.

"To Daniel, our Captain!"

The room erupted in applause, celebrating not just the completion of the project but the ownership that made it happen.

For the first time in days, Daniel exhaled fully, sinking into a beanbag chair.

He realised then: *Accountability doesn't just deliver results. It also creates trust, loyalty, and a culture of courage.*

4. The Defining Moment: A Second Crisis

Hours before the final investor demo, the system suffered a last-minute glitch.

The AI-driven analytics tool froze, its algorithm failing to process real-time data.

The team stared at flickering error screens.

Marcus paced the room while Mei Ling whispered into a phone, trying to reach the Estonian developers.

All eyes turned to Daniel.

The choice before Daniel was brutal:

1. Run a backup version, sacrificing the most impressive features.

2. Patch it up live, and take the enormous risk that the demo could crash in front of investors.

Daniel took a deep breath, steadying himself.

"Everything I've done so far has led to this moment. The demo is our final test; if I play it safe now, all the effort will be wasted."

He closed his eyes for a second.

"We'll patch it live. I'll own whatever happens."

5. The Demo Room

The conference room at the Armani Hotel, Burj Khalifa, was sleek and sophisticated. A massive screen dominated the space, showcasing the AI-powered fintech tool.

Investors from London, Singapore, and New York sat at a polished mahogany table, their expressions sharp with expectation.

Daniel operated the demo himself.

As the real-time data streamed in, the system froze.

For a single, suffocating moment, there was a pin-drop silence.

And then, it worked.

The AI model kicked in, displaying flawless insights.

Investors leaned forward, exchanging impressed glances.

When the demo ended, the room erupted in applause.

Marcus walked over, shaking Daniel's hand firmly.

"You didn't just fix a problem. You took control of it. That's leadership."

One investor approached Marcus during the tea that followed.

"We've rarely seen this level of ownership in action. It's inspiring."

6. The Quiet Victory

The startup secured multi-million-dollar funding, and Daniel's contributions were widely recognised.

Marcus offered him a permanent leadership role in the company.

But what mattered to Daniel most wasn't his title, but the respect that he earned.

The team started calling him "Captain Daniel," not for his position, but for the moment he took the wheel when no one else dared.

Accountability isn't about carrying the burden alone. It's about stepping up when others hesitate, creating trust, and building momentum.

Like the **Blacktip Shark**, Daniel owned his moment, and it transformed his career.

Blacktip Shark Lesson: Own Zone

- ✓ Don't wait for conditions to be perfect.
- ✓ Move fast, make decisions with precision, and own the outcome—whether good or bad.

As you reflect on Daniel's journey, consider this:

Where in your life are you hesitating to take ownership of a challenge?

What is that bold decision that you could make to inspire those around you?

Imagine yourself as the Blacktip Shark: precise, agile, and unafraid to thrive in chaos. How can you channel this mindset to make a difference today?

Blacktip Shark Exercise: Learn to Own It & to Lead It

Do This Right Away: Take responsibility for a task or project that is not showing signs of progress. Identify a part of the task or project that feels stuck. Take ownership by clearly defining its next steps and leading its execution. Repeat this step till completion of the project.

Do This on Completion of the Task/Project: Reflect on how taking ownership influenced the outcome and your team's trust in you.

Real-World Example: How Satya Nadella Led Change through Accountability

1. The Sluggish Phase

Before **Satya Nadella** took over as CEO of Microsoft in 2014, the company was facing an identity crisis. Microsoft was still a tech giant, but it had lost its edge and innovation.

Under former CEO Steve Ballmer, the company had focused heavily on Windows and legacy software, while rivals like Apple, Google, and Amazon surged ahead in cloud computing, mobile, and AI.

Employees described Microsoft's culture as competitive, bureaucratic, and internally divided, with a lack of accountability and agility.

Satya Nadella had been with Microsoft since 1992, leading cloud-computing initiatives, but he wasn't yet seen as a transformational leader.

2. Taking Charge, Bringing Change

When Nadella was appointed CEO in 2014, the stakes couldn't have been higher:

- Microsoft's mobile strategy had failed, with the Nokia acquisition turning into a disaster.
- Cloud computing was taking over, but Microsoft's Windows-first approach was slowing its adoption.

The company was seen as stuck in the past, focusing on products instead of innovation and customer needs.

Instead of blaming past leadership or making slow, cautious moves, Nadella fully owned Microsoft's challenges. He brought the **Blacktip Shark** mindset of embracing accountability, cutting through bureaucracy, and making bold moves.

3. Making Accountability Felt

As CEO, Nadella didn't waste time making tough decisions:

- ✓ **Embraced Cloud-First**: He shifted Microsoft's focus from Windows-centric to Cloud and AI-driven, betting big on Azure.
- ✓ **Dismantled Internal Silos**: He promoted collaboration over competition, breaking the culture of internal rivalries.
- ✓ **Killed Failing Strategies**: He ended Microsoft's mobile ambitions, writing off the $7.6 billion Nokia acquisition and focusing on what Microsoft did best: software, cloud, and AI.
- ✓ **Promoted Growth Mindset**: Instead of blaming past failures, he made accountability the core of Microsoft's culture, inspiring employees to learn, take ownership, and drive change.

Many doubted his empathetic leadership approach, arguing that tech giants thrive on cutthroat competition. But Nadella proved that accountability combined with innovation creates lasting success.

4. How Microsoft Transformed

Under Nadella's leadership, Microsoft transformed from a slow-moving corporate giant to an innovation powerhouse:

- ✓ **Stock Price Skyrocketed**: Microsoft's market value tripled under Nadella, reaching over $2 trillion.
- ✓ **Azure Became a Cloud Leader**: Microsoft's cloud business went from an afterthought to a dominant force, competing head-to-head with Amazon Web Services (AWS).
- ✓ **Shifted to Subscription-Based Model**: He revamped Microsoft's business model, and as a result, Office 365 and cloud-based services became the company's growth engine.
- ✓ **Cultural Shift at Microsoft**: Employees reported a more open, collaborative, and accountable work culture, moving away from the past "blame game" mindset.

Satya Nadella's transformation of Microsoft was not about luck. It was about owning challenges, making bold decisions, and holding himself and the company accountable.

It's Time for You to Step Forward!

"Be the Blacktip Shark. Claim your domain, embrace accountability, and inspire leadership through decisive actions."

Swimming Ahead for the Next Shark

Ownership is powerful, but leadership isn't just about making quick decisions. Some challenges require persistence, resilience, and the ability to endure setbacks. Now, let's dive into the world of the **Whale Shark**, the master of long-term vision.

Chapter 5: The Whale Shark – Patience & Persistence

Meet the Whale Shark

Scientific Name: *Rhincodon typus*

Habitat: Open, tropical oceans, often solitary but sometimes seen in groups.

Behaviour: Gentle and enduring, the Whale Shark is the largest fish in the ocean, known for its calm demeanour and long journeys.

Unique Trait: Persistence through slow, steady and purposeful movement.

With patience and persistence, the Whale Shark moves steadily towards its goals.

Story: "Slow, Steady, Unstoppable Faisal"

1. The Relentless Climb

The sun blazed mercilessly over the Moroccan desert as Faisal wiped the sweat from his brow. He wasn't here for adventure, but to make history. A young entrepreneur from Casablanca, Faisal had spent the last five years building his solar energy startup, SunEdge, with a mission to bring **renewable power** to remote African villages.

His company had reached a breaking point. Despite years of hard work, partnerships were failing, investors were hesitant, and government bureaucracy was a never-ending maze. His biggest setback? A massive solar farm project in Senegal was on the verge of collapse due to delayed permits.

Standing before his prototype, a towering solar panel array, he sighed. "We're running out of time," he muttered.

2. The Endless Setbacks

Every path forward seemed blocked.

- Bureaucratic hurdles meant months of waiting for project approvals.
- Major investors pulled out, claiming the project was too slow-moving.
- Local suppliers failed to deliver, delaying construction further.

The pressure mounted. Faisal's team dwindled, demotivated by the constant delays. One by one, they left for more stable jobs. Even his co-founder, Karim, had doubts.

"Maybe it's time to cut our losses," Karim suggested one evening. "The market isn't ready."

Faisal clenched his jaw. Every fibre of his being wanted to walk away and start fresh. But deep down, he knew the world wouldn't change unless someone refused to quit.

3. Enter the Whale Shark Moment

One evening, after another investor rejection, Faisal found himself watching a documentary on whale sharks. The narrator described how these gentle giants swim thousands of miles, never hunting in bursts, filtering plankton tirelessly from gallons of water to sustain themselves, never stopping, always moving forward.

Endurance was the key.

Faisal realised: *Persistence wasn't about quick victories. It was about staying the course despite the storm.*

Instead of chasing massive wins, he focused on smaller, steady progress:

- ✓ **Redefining the goal:** Instead of a full-scale launch, he started small, bringing solar power to just one village in Senegal.
- ✓ **Building momentum:** A viral video showcasing the impact of the pilot project caught the attention of NGOs.
- ✓ **Leveraging alternative funding:** Crowdfunding campaigns and microloans replaced lost investors.

Like the **Whale Shark** filtering the ocean, Faisal learned to find opportunity in persistence.

4. The Breaking Point

Just as things were looking up, disaster struck. A key government contract was revoked due to an internal policy change, slashing funding for rural solar projects. It felt like the final blow.

“We’re done,” Karim said. “We have nothing left.”

Faisal refused to believe it. Instead of retreating, he went public and launched a social media campaign that caught fire. Climate activists, journalists, and global influencers picked up his story. Within a month, a new coalition of African entrepreneurs rallied behind SunEdge, offering private funding and strategic partnerships.

5. The Big Payoff

A year later, Faisal stood at the opening ceremony of SunEdge’s first fully operational solar farm, lighting up over 10,000 homes. The vast field of solar panels stretched across the Senegalese plains, shimmering under the relentless sun. The once-barren land now pulsed with activity:

- ✓ Technicians fine-tuning the installations
- ✓ Children curiously inspecting the panels
- ✓ Families witnessing their homes glow with electricity for the first time

The surroundings buzzed with transformation. Small businesses, including tailors, barbershops, and food stalls, sprang up, no longer constrained by darkness. At night, streetlights illuminated winding roads that once vanished into the shadows. It wasn’t just a power project; it was a movement.

Karim, standing beside him, grinned. “You never gave up, did you?”

Faisal smiled. “The Whale Shark never stops swimming.”

6. The 'Persistence Reward'

Months later, Faisal returned to Senegal to check on their earliest solar-powered village. Children played under streetlights that never used to work. Elders gathered in homes no longer trapped in darkness.

And that's when he observed something amazing. A small local entrepreneur had started a business charging mobile phones using SunEdge's solar panels.

He then realised that persistence wasn't just about enduring. *It was about outlasting the challenges until the world caught up to the vision.*

Whale Shark Lesson: Persistence Principle

- ✓ Those who persist don't just survive; they create an ecosystem where others thrive.
- ✓ Stay steady. Grow Silently.

Take a moment to reflect:

- **Where in your life are you facing a challenge** that feels overwhelming or endless?
- **Have you considered giving up** recently? Why?
- **What's that one small, consistent action** you can take today, even if the results aren't immediate?

Whale Shark Exercise: Understanding the Power of Patience and Persistence

Do This Today: Commit to a long-term goal or project that is important for you. Break your goal into three smaller, manageable steps, and take the first step today.

Do This Over the Next Few Days: Reflect on how completing a small step helped reinforce your commitment to the larger goal.

Real-World Example: Nelson Mandela's Patience That Changed a Nation

1. The Angry, Young Man Phase

Nelson Mandela was a young activist fighting against apartheid in South Africa before he became the global symbol of perseverance and unity.

As a leader of the African National Congress (ANC) in the 1950s and 1960s, he was determined to dismantle racial segregation, which oppressed Black South Africans under a brutally enforced system.

Early in his activism, Mandela believed that change could happen swiftly through mass protests and direct resistance.

However, the South African government responded with violent crackdowns, forcing Mandela into hiding and, eventually, leading to his arrest in 1962.

At this stage, Mandela was a fighter, but he hadn't yet embraced the deep patience of the **Whale Shark**.

2. The Realisation (BYOS Moment)

In 1964, Nelson Mandela was sentenced to life imprisonment for his activism.

He was sent to Robben Island, a maximum-security prison, where he was confined in harsh conditions of a tiny cell, where he was forced to labour in limestone quarries, with little contact with the outside world.

At first, anger and frustration burned within him, but Mandela soon realised that rage alone wouldn't dismantle apartheid.

He began thinking long-term, adopting the Whale Shark's patience: steadfast, slow-moving, but unstoppable in its path.

Mandela realised that change wouldn't come from immediate rebellion but from patience, strategy, and unshakable endurance.

3. The Real Transformation

While in prison for twenty-seven years, Mandela transformed himself and the anti-apartheid movement:

- ✓ He refused to give in to despair, focusing on self-education, learning law and writing letters to keep the movement alive.
- ✓ He secretly negotiated with the government, understanding that confrontation alone wouldn't lead to lasting change.
- ✓ He became a symbol of hope for millions, proving that persistence, and not speed, was the key to winning the fight against apartheid.
- ✓ He used his patience strategically by working towards gradual reconciliation to prevent civil war rather than pushing for immediate, radical change.

Many of his fellow activists wanted faster, more aggressive action, but Mandela remained steadfast like the Whale Shark, understanding that real change required decades of effort, not just moments of passion.

4. Finally, The Outcome

In 1990, after twenty-seven years in prison, Mandela was finally released.

Instead of seeking revenge, he promoted reconciliation, ensuring that South Africa did not fall into chaos.

He led negotiations that dismantled apartheid, proving that patience and diplomacy were stronger than oppression.

In 1994, he became South Africa's first Black president, guiding the country towards democracy through unity, not division.

He spent the rest of his life advocating for peace, reinforcing that long-term success requires persistence, resilience, and a vision beyond one's lifetime.

Mandela's leadership was a masterclass in patience. He didn't react to oppression with immediate retaliation. Instead, he outlasted it, wearing down the system like the slow, steady force of the Whale Shark.

Be the Change You Wish Around You!

"Are you chasing quick wins, or are you patiently building systems for long-term change? Be the Whale Shark - steady, focused, and persistent."

The Journey Continues

Patience is key to long-term success, but life isn't always predictable. Sometimes, things change fast, and waiting isn't an option.

The ability to pivot and adapt is what defines true resilience. Turn the page over to find out how the **Tiger Shark** embodies resilience.

The Dilemma that Stays...

Not all victories come from pushing harder. Some come when you flow with the current rather than against it. But how do you recognise when to persist and when to trust the flow? Ah, trust! We'll explore that soon...

Chapter 6:
The Tiger Shark – The Power of the Pivot

Meet the Tiger Shark

Scientific Name: *Galeocerdo cuvier*

Habitat: Tropical and temperate waters worldwide.

Behaviour: Bold, curious scavengers who adapt through sudden, decisive pivots when opportunity or challenge appears

Unique Trait: Known for extreme versatility; able to change course instantly in response to new conditions.

The Tiger Shark doesn't fear uncertainty; it responds by utilising its razor-sharp ability to pivot the instant the ocean shifts.

Story: "Kabir's Adaptability in the Unknown"

1. A Journey into the Unknown

The **Great Nicobar Island** was as beautiful as it was brutal; a dense, breathing world of emerald forests, tangled mangroves, and unpredictable waterways. For Kabir, a young environmentalist and researcher, it also presented the most daunting challenge of his career.

Tasked with leading a team of seasoned ecologists and volunteers into an endangered and previously unexplored mangrove ecosystem, Kabir was thrilled but nervous. The assignment required precision and adaptability, qualities he was still trying to master.

Their destination was Crocodile Creek near the 41st milestone, a site notorious for its unpredictable tides and wildlife.

The trek through the dense, marshy forest began with high spirits.

Kabir reminded himself of his supervisor's parting words: "This isn't a regular research trip, Kabir. This is about navigating the unexpected. Stay sharp and adapt quickly as challenges unfold." He quickly identified the importance of remaining flexible, mapping alternative plans in his mind even as they marched forward.

The forest waited ahead, silent and watching.

2. The Storm Unleashed

As the group pushed forward, the canopy darkened and the marshland deepened.

Every step was a negotiation with sinking mud and shifting ground.

That's when Amrita froze.

Two glowing eyes stared back from the swamp.

Crocodiles. Crocodiles!

"We need to turn back," a volunteer whispered.

Kabir felt it too—the instinct to retreat.

But another instinct rose stronger: pivot.

"Not back," he said. "Sideways. Follow me." It wasn't the safest option. It wasn't the planned one.

But at that moment, it was the only viable pivot.

The team turned sharply into a parallel route: dense, thorny, but away from the reptiles' line of movement.

For the first time, Kabir understood something vital:

Adaptability isn't always graceful. Sometimes, it's a sharp turn made in seconds.

3. The Swamp Awakens

As they progressed, the terrain worsened. Rahul, a junior member, misstepped and sank waist-deep into the mud.

"Help!" shouted Rahul, his quivering voice filled with terror. The murky water rippled as the crocodiles stirred nearby.

As fear gripped Kabir momentarily, he drew a lesson from his past failure: Don't freeze. Don't overthink; just read the situation and pivot instinctively.

He recalibrated quickly.

"Everyone, stay calm! Amrita, hand me the rope! Now!"

Within moments, they formed a human chain, pulled Rahul to safety, and shifted direction again to higher ground. The narrow escape left everyone shaken but alive.

This was not the plan.

This was not even Plan B.

This was "pivot, or perish."

And Kabir was beginning to understand that survival in uncertainty required fast directional changes, not flawless execution of a rigid plan.

4. Enter the Tiger Shark

Tiger sharks are bold, opportunistic, and capable of sudden directional changes when hunting. They adapt by changing course quickly when they sense opportunity or threat.

Kabir didn't have the perfect plan. But like the Tiger Shark, he had to trust his ability to pivot.

"We'll build a bamboo bridge across the marsh," he announced. "It's the only way to cross the swamp safely."

The team hesitated. Doubt was written on their faces. "Trust me," Kabir urged. "We can do this together."

The team exchanged uncertain glances. Amrita voiced what they were all thinking. "Do we even have the time or the tools for this?"

Kabir's voice remained steady, "We don't have another option. Use bamboo, vines, and anything sturdy we can find."

The team's makeshift bridge began to take shape under the fading light. They split bamboo poles and secured them with tightly wound vines. The structure swayed precariously with each piece added, but Kabir's steady commands kept the group focused.

"One step at a time," he reminded them, his voice cutting through the rising panic.

As the first volunteer tested the bridge, it creaked ominously.

"Keep going," Kabir urged, his voice firm despite his own mounting anxiety. "This is our way forward."

One by one, the team crossed the bamboo bridge, moving cautiously but steadily.

Kabir crossed last, feeling the thrill and exhaustion of a man who had just made three critical pivots in a day.

5. Lost in the Jungle

Hours later, as the team continued through the dense forest, the terrain grew more treacherous. Thick undergrowth blocked their path, and their navigation devices were useless.

Kabir glanced at the weary team, sweat streaking their faces. The morale (that had surged after the swamp victory) was fading fast.

Time for another pivot.

"We're not stopping," Kabir said firmly. "We head toward higher ground. If we get above the tree line, we can signal for help."

The team moved cautiously, using machetes to clear the way. Every step felt heavier as night fell, and the forest erupted with unfamiliar, eerie sounds.

Kabir tightened his grip on the machete. "Nothing we can't handle." But his heart raced as he thought of the **Tiger Shark** again. It didn't panic in the face of danger; it pivoted.

6. The Helicopter Rescue

At dawn, the group finally reached a clearing on a rocky outcrop. Kabir and Amrita quickly assembled a makeshift signal fire using dry twigs and leaves.

"This has to work," Kabir muttered as they lit the fire. Flames roared upward, and they waved their flashlights in wide arcs to attract attention.

Nothing. Minutes crawled by.

Then—a distant hum!

A helicopter appeared over the ridge.

"They've seen us!" Amrita shouted, her face lighting up with relief.

The helicopter hovered above and dropped a rescue harness. There were exhausted but triumphant smiles.

Kabir exhaled deeply, realising how far they had come, not by sticking to a plan, but by changing direction every time the moment demanded it.

7. A New Day

Back at their base camp near Galathea Bay, after their debriefing, Rahul approached Kabir.

"Thanks for saving me back there," he said quietly. "I don't know how you stayed so calm."

Amrita stopped and looked up at Kabir expectantly.

Kabir smiled, though the weight of the day still lingered. "I wasn't calm," he admitted. "I just kept pivoting."

As Kabir sat by the fire that evening, he replayed the journey in his mind: the swamp, the storm, the lost GPS signal.

Every danger.

Every fork.

Every failure of the original plan.

All of them had forced a turn.

A sharp, decisive, necessary turn.

Just like the Tiger Shark.

True adaptability is not about avoiding disruption, but about mastering the art of pivoting under pressure.

Tiger Shark Insight: Shift Sense

✓ Thrive in the unknown.

✓ Turn Fast. Adjust Boldly. Pivot with Purpose.

What about you? Have there been uncertain moments when your original plan fell apart, making you think about what to do next?

Where in your life are you hesitating to pivot because of fear of failure or the unknown?

The swamp taught Kabir this truth: uncertainty isn't a dead end but an invitation to pivot. And perhaps, it can teach you the same.

Tiger Shark Exercise: Learning to Adapt and Act

Write Down Now: Recall a recent situation where your original plan fell apart. What immediate adjustments did you make? If you froze, what would you do differently next time?

Think and Write: How did/would adapting quickly in a difficult situation change your outcome?

Real-World Example: Sully, the Hero of the Hudson

1. When Routine was a Comfort

Before **Captain Chesley "Sully" Sullenberger** became a household name, he was a seasoned US Air Force pilot and a highly experienced commercial airline captain.

He had thousands of flight hours under his belt, handling aircrafts in various conditions.

While he was skilled, his flights were usually routine: following strict protocols, trained for emergencies, but never expecting the unimaginable.

At this stage, he was well-experienced, but he hadn't yet been in a situation that would demand him to "think out of the box".

He had never faced a real-life scenario where every second meant life or death.

Life had been a smooth curve. Until January 15, 2009.

2. The Crisis Situation: Also, the Ultimate test

On January 15, 2009, Sully was piloting US Airways Flight 1549 when, just minutes after take-off, both engines failed due to a bird strike.

Altitude? Too low.

Time to react? Less than 200 seconds.

Options? Almost none.

The turning point? In a fraction of a second, Sully had to abandon conventional thinking and embrace **Tiger Shark** instincts—fast, aggressive, fearless adaptation.

3. Crash or Pivot: Sully's BYOS Moment

Instead of panicking or following rigid protocols, Sully immediately pivoted:

- ✓ Ruled out returning to the airport as there wasn't enough altitude.
- ✓ Assessed nearby landing spots and realised none were viable.
- ✓ Made a near-impossible decision by landing in the icy Hudson River, a move no manual recommended.

- ✓ Communicated with precision by telling the passengers and the crew to brace for impact while executing a textbook-perfect water landing.

This was the Tiger Shark in action: thinking on the move, pivotingg, and executing in the heat of chaos.

4. Sully Took His Chance and Succeeded

- ✓ Every single one of the 155 passengers survived.
- ✓ The landing was hailed as the "Miracle on the Hudson."
- ✓ His decision-making under extreme pressure became a case study in adaptability and leadership.
- ✓ He redefined crisis management, showing that true leadership isn't about sticking to the manual, but knowing when to throw the manual out and trust your instincts.

Sully's actions proved that in high-stakes situations, overthinking leads to disaster: only a swift, fearless pivot action saves the day.

Now, it's Your Turn!

"When the path forward is not clear, do not freeze. Do not wait. Turn. Pivot. Be the Tiger Shark."

Moving Beyond Survival: The Power of Evolution, Stillness, and Power

Adapting to change is crucial, but true transformation comes when we evolve, innovate, and break free from old patterns.

Part 3 of this book will now present the next set of sharks who will guide you through transformation, resilience, and leadership mastery.

Part 3: Leading with Strength

True leadership is built on self-awareness, resilience, and the courage to take charge. These sharks guide you toward becoming the leader your team needs.

Discover Your Shark Quiz - 3

Identify whether you need the **Zebra Shark**, the **Nurse Shark** or the **Great White Shark.**

Answer the questions below with Yes or No:

1. **Do you often neglect self-care** while focusing on goals?
2. **Do complicated or chaotic situations** tend to **put you off balance**?
3. **Do you get uncomfortable** when pushed into **high-stakes** leadership **situations**?

Check if you find your shark(s) below:

- **Yes to Question 1**: You need a **Nurse Shark** to build inner strength to endure long-term challenges (**Resilience**).
- **Yes to Question 2**: Bring a **Zebra Shark** to help you reflect on yourself and evolve your perspective (**Self-Awareness**).
- **Yes to Question 3**: Befriend the **Great White Shark** to learn how to command authority and make bold decisions (**Leadership Mastery**).

Chapter 7:
The Zebra Shark – The Art of Manoeuvring

Meet the Zebra Shark

Scientific Name: *Stegostoma tigrinum*

Habitat: Coral reefs, shallow waters, complex ocean terrains

Behaviour: Calm, patient navigators who adapt through slow, fluid manoeuvring in tight and complex spaces.

Unique Trait: Exceptional at slipping through narrow gaps, making subtle course corrections, and navigating labyrinths without panic or speed.

Unlike the Tiger Shark, which thrives on sharp pivots, the Zebra Shark succeeds through fluid manoeuvring. It relies on reading the terrain, making micro-adjustments, and adjusting continuously until a path emerges.

Story: "Ravi's New Rules for Survival"

1. The Corporate Cage

Ravi, in his mid-fifties, sat in his dimly lit corner cubicle of a bustling corporate office in Mumbai's Central Business District. The walls were adorned with sticky notes, a faded family photo, and a certificate of "Employee of the Year" from eight years ago; the faint hum of the old air conditioning mixed with the distant chatter of young, energetic colleagues.

Ravi's days spent in the office weren't miserable, but they weren't exciting either. One routine blurred into the next, creating a loop of meetings, emails, and pivot tables held together by cups of coffee.

He often scrolled through stories of people reinventing their careers in their fifties but dismissed them as "not for me."

Ravi scrolled through an unopened email from HR titled, "Upskilling Opportunities for Senior Managers." He sighed. Around him, younger colleagues talked about AI, automation. He wasn't miserable, just stagnant.

"I have been here for two decades, but where do I go now?" he thought as he sipped his lukewarm tea.

2. Enter the Zebra Shark

Priya, Ravi's manager, a sharp, no-nonsense leader in her late thirties, passed by.

"Ravi, have you considered that digital course HR circulated? Might give you fresh perspectives."

Ravi forced a smile but felt the knot tighten in his stomach.

That day at home, over dinner, Ravi's teenage daughter asked, **"Dad, what would you do if money weren't a problem?"**

Her innocent question lingered in his mind long after the lights were turned off.

And for the first time, Ravi sensed that he didn't need to flip his life upside down. He only needed to take one gentle turn.

Just like the Zebra Shark, which begins life with stripes and slowly evolves into spots, Ravi wasn't changing who he was.

He was manoeuvring into who he could become. One Friday afternoon, during a company leadership workshop, a guest speaker, a former colleague, now the CEO of another firm, took the stage.

"Adaptability isn't jumping into the unknown. It's preparing step by step, so you're ready when the opportunity knocks."

The speaker's words stirred something deep inside Ravi. For the first time, he acknowledged the need to learn.

That night, while staring at his email inbox, Ravi clicked on the "Digital Transformation for Leaders" course link.

He enrolled.

Just as the **Zebra Shark** thrives by adapting to unknown challenges, Ravi's ability to evolve in his corporate environment reflects this powerful trait of embracing change with resilience.

3. Moments of Doubt: Learning to Manoeuvre Slowly

For the first few weeks, Ravi struggled.

The interface felt alien. The jargon was overwhelming. His confidence wavered every time he joined an online discussion with younger, tech-savvy peers.

One module focused on "Design Thinking: Customer Journey Mapping and Persona Creation." Ravi had to create a customer journey map for a hypothetical client.

"Customer personas? Journey stages? I'm not a marketing guy," Ravi muttered under his breath as he tried piecing together the assignment, watching video tutorials repeatedly. His progress was glacial.

Just as he was about to hit the "Withdraw from Course" button, he received a ping from a peer in the discussion forum.

"Hey, Ravi! Want to collaborate on this exercise? I struggled too, but we can crack it together."

Ravi said yes.

He didn't pivot.

He adjusted.

He watched the videos again.

Took notes.

Submitted assignments.

Improved his customer persona map with help.

Micro-adjustments.

Micro-wins.

Micro-confidence. "I can do this," Ravi thought, a faint smile forming on his lips.

Next came Agile Methodologies. The module talked about sprints, backlogs, retrospectives, and stand-ups. But this time, he pushed himself to rethink his approach.

He reflected, "Ravi, you've been in this company for two decades now, accepting and embracing so many changes. You already know agility; you just didn't have the jargon for it. Give yourself some credit."

The next day, he manoeuvred through the unfamiliar concepts and cross-referenced them with real-life office scenarios. Slowly, things started to click.

During the next sprint retrospective exercise, Ravi confidently presented his insights on workflow prioritisation, earning appreciative nods from his peers.

4. Reflection: Understanding the Shark Within

On a rainy evening, Ravi sat by the office window, droplets sliding down the glass. He watched a documentary on the **Zebra Sharks** and noticed how they navigate reefs.

Not through sudden turns...

But through gentle adjustments.

Not through force...

But through reading the terrain.

That's when it clicked:

Adaptation doesn't always come from big moves. Sometimes, it emerges from small, intentional manoeuvres.

The **Zebra Shark** had shown him the way.

5. The Turning Point: Breaking the Cycle

Energised, Ravi completed his Digital Transformation course with distinction. Inspired, he enrolled in an Environmental, Social, and Governance (ESG) Compliance Training.

The Carbon Emissions Calculation Methodology pushed Ravi to his limit. The formulas, emission scopes, and data mapping overwhelmed him.

He smiled faintly. "It's hard, but I'll figure it out."

Ravi began breaking down the problem and did the following:

- ✓ Approached it systematically, focusing on one formula at a time.
- ✓ Cross-referenced industry reports.
- ✓ Asked questions in the discussion forum.

When the assignment results were published, Ravi had not only passed but had the second-highest score in his cohort.

The knot of self-doubt slowly began to loosen.

6. The Payoff: Small Steps, Big Shifts

Over the next year:

- ✓ Ravi completed two more certifications.
- ✓ He began mentoring younger team members on compliance and automation tools.
- ✓ His insights were referenced in leadership meetings.

One afternoon, an email landed in his inbox: "We are pleased to offer you the role of Senior Consultant – Digital and ESG Initiatives."

Ravi stared at the screen, tears welling up in his eyes.

That night, his daughter asked again, "Dad, what would you do if money weren't a problem?"

This time, he answered with a smile: "Exactly what I'm doing now."

Ravi's transformation was complete.

Zebra Shark Insight: The Adaptive Edge

- ✓ You don't need to always change the direction of the ship to reach new horizons. Sometimes, you just need to adjust your sails.

✓ Manoeuvre quietly. Evolve Fully.

The **Zebra Shark** represents the ability to manoeuvre with resilience, and incremental change.

True transformation doesn't always require grand gestures; it begins with small, micro manoeuvres. Are there areas in your life where you feel stuck in routine? What's one small change you can make today to manoeuvre towards growth?

Zebra Shark Exercise: Learning to Manoeuvre Gently

Do This Today: Address an area where you feel stuck. Identify one small, actionable change you can make today to create momentum in that area.

Do This Later: Observe how these micro-adjustments accumulate into major shifts.

Real-World Example: How Beyoncé Made Reinvention a Way of Life

1. Queen in the Cocoon, Waiting to Grow Her Wings

Early in her singing career, **Beyoncé** was the lead singer of Destiny's Child, one of the best-selling girl groups in history.

She was known for her powerful voice, stage presence, and disciplined work ethic. But as part of a group, she was confined within a collective identity, sharing the spotlight and creative direction.

While Destiny's Child was a global success, Beyoncé had bigger ambitions: to evolve, experiment, and redefine music on her own terms.

At this point, she was a superstar, but not yet an icon of reinvention.

2. The Gamble Paid Off

In 2003, Beyoncé took the biggest risk of her career by going solo!

Leaving a successful group meant venturing into the unknown.

Many questioned whether she could succeed on her own or if she would fade like other former group singers.

But Beyoncé wasn't just stepping out. She was reinventing herself completely.

She released *Dangerously in Love*, proving that she wasn't just a singer, but a force of nature with her own artistic vision.

3. When Evolution became a Norm

Since then, Beyoncé has continuously transformed, just like the **Zebra Shark**, which changes its patterns as it matures:

- ✓ She never played it safe; every album had a distinct sound and creative direction.
- ✓ She defied industry norms by dropping her album unexpectedly on iTunes in 2013 without any promotions or marketing. The surprise release was an unprecedented success.
- ✓ She embraced multimedia storytelling, turning albums into cinematic experiences (*Lemonade*, *Black Is King*).
- ✓ She took full creative control, proving that true artistry isn't just about talent; it's about vision, innovation, and adaptability.

Instead of riding trends, she created them, evolving with every project while staying true to herself.

4. And the Results Followed

- ✓ Beyoncé became the most awarded female artist in Grammy history.
- ✓ She built a billion-dollar brand, expanding into fashion (Ivy Park), film, and activism.
- ✓ She redefined what it means to be an independent artist, owning her masters and controlling her narrative.
- ✓ She never became predictable. Every era of Beyoncé feels fresh, unique, and ahead of its time.

Beyoncé's success isn't about luck or talent alone. It's about constant evolution, reinvention, and the courage to embrace change.

Time to Make Your Move Now!

"Be Bold yet Gentle. Be Relentless yet Observant. Be Unstoppable yet Steady."

Heading into Deeper Waters

Breaking free is liberating, but sometimes, the real power lies in stillness. What if your strength doesn't come from action and speed, but comes from resilience and quiet confidence?

In the next chapter, the **Nurse Shark** will show you why sometimes, still waters run the deepest.

Chapter 8:
The Nurse Shark – Strength in Stillness

Meet the Nurse Shark

Scientific Name: *Ginglymostoma cirratum*

Habitat: Warm, shallow coastal waters often resting on sandy ocean floors.

Behaviour: Calm and unassuming, Nurse Sharks display incredible patience and endurance.

Unique Trait: Known for their calm demeanour and emotional control, waiting for the perfect moment to act.

In stillness, the Nurse Shark finds strength and clarity.

Story: "How Amrit Drew her Strength from Pausing"

1. The Calm before the Storm

It was a crisp, breezy morning in Vancouver, with the city waking up to the shimmering waters of the Pacific. Amrit Gill, a senior marketing manager at **NorthStar Enterprises**, hurried into the office, her mind racing through her agenda for the day.

The boardroom buzzed with energy. Amrit leaned forward, taking meticulous notes as her colleagues presented ideas for an upcoming campaign. But as the discussion intensified, a dull ache spread across her forehead. She shook it off, attributing it to stress.

Then, without warning, a sharp, searing pain erupted.

"Amrit!" her colleague, Lisa, exclaimed, noticing her slump forward. Chaos erupted as Lisa dialled for an ambulance while another teammate steadied her trembling hand. Within minutes, paramedics whisked Amrit to St. Paul's Hospital, leaving her team in stunned silence. Amrit's husband, Harjeet, arrived at the hospital in a frenzy.

2. The Crisis

The doctor's words felt surreal: "A ruptured brain aneurysm. She's stable but needs immediate surgery."

The hours crawled by as Harjeet waited anxiously. Finally, the surgeon emerged. "The procedure went well, but recovery would require rest, therapy, and patience. Resilience will be key," he said. Harjeet nodded, silently vowing to be her anchor through the storm.

Amrit closed her eyes briefly. The word aneurysm echoed in her mind. "I should've seen the signs," she murmured.

Harjeet leaned closer; his voice was soft but firm. "No one could've predicted this, Amrit. But we're here now, and we'll take one step at a time."

A week later, during a follow-up angioplasty, a critical error occurred. A catheter punctured the wrong artery, causing internal bleeding in the abdomen, and Amrit's pulse dropped dangerously low. Machines beeped wildly, and one more emergency intervention was launched.

As Amrit stabilised in the ICU, Harjeet was a worried man. When they finally met after twenty-four hours, he was surprised to find Amrit smiling. She held his hand and said, "This too shall pass."

3. The Recovery: A Symbol of Persistence

Days turned into weeks. The world outside moved on, but Amrit's recovery was slow. Therapy was gruelling. Each small movement felt monumental.

- Mornings began with stretching exercises in her small corner room.
- Afternoons were spent in guided therapy sessions.
- Evenings included slow walks around Stanley Park, with Harjeet holding her hand every step of the way.

Yet, every small win felt like a victory.

4. The Recovery Begins: The Nurse Shark Emerges

That night, staring out of the hospital window at Vancouver's skyline, Amrit leaned back in the chair. She realised:

Calmness isn't just a state of mind. It's a powerful tool to guide you through fear and uncertainty.

Unlike their fierce cousins, **Nurse Sharks** don't rely on speed or aggression to survive. They are patient, calculated, and masters of sensing their environment.

Their specialised barbels, whisker-like sensory organs near their mouths, help them detect and locate prey even in total darkness, sweeping the ocean floor methodically before making a move.

Amrit's recovery was no different. She couldn't rush the process and had to be patient, sensing progress even when it wasn't visible.

Slowly but steadily, she improved. Each step was proof of her resilience:

✓ Walked to the window without support.

✓ Talked to a colleague on the phone.

✓ Participated in a short online session.

"Recovery is a slow process," her therapist would remind her.

Amrit realised that growth wasn't about sudden bursts of strength but about quiet persistence; just like the **Nurse Shark** using its barbels to navigate, trusting that progress would come step by step.

5. Returning to Life

After three months, Amrit was discharged. But recovery didn't stop there.

Every morning, she would sit by Stanley Park's Seawall, watching joggers and cyclists pass by. She wasn't there to envy them. She was there to breathe, to absorb the energy of life around her.

One evening, sitting at the Seawall, Harjeet turned to her and said: "You know, you've become softer, yet stronger. Like still water with the strength of a tide beneath it."

Amrit smiled. She had learned that resilience doesn't roar; it thrives in stillness, in sensing progress when it isn't immediately visible.

6. Sharing the Journey

As Amrit settled into her routine, she began mentoring younger colleagues. She shared her experience openly, emphasising the importance of resilience and self-care.

One colleague, Aisha, approached her after a session. "Amrit, your story inspired me. I've been struggling with burnout, but your advice gives me hope."

Amrit smiled, realising that in a world that moves fast, stillness is a superpower. The **Nurse Shark** thrives by knowing when to pause, recover, and then strike when the moment is right.

Amrit's strength was in her ability to remain composed in a moment of crisis.

Nurse Shark Insight: Silent Fortitude

- ✓ Find strength in calm, resilience in stillness, and clarity in composure.
- ✓ Lead quietly. Anchor Deeply.

Now it's your turn to embrace calm resilience.

- **How often do you rush** to see results, forgetting that growth happens in the unseen moments?
- **Do you dismiss your quiet, personal victories**, or do you honour them as steps toward something greater?

- **What small habits can you** develop to stay composed under pressure?

Nurse Shark Exercise: Build a Habit of Calm under Stress

Do This Now: Recall a stressful moment this week. Write three ways you could have paused and responded with calmness.

Do This Later: Practise giving a pause when under stress. Reflect on how intentional calmness affects your ability to navigate stress.

Real-World Example: Jacinda Ardern's Quiet Leadership in Adversity

1. Accomplished Yet Unproven

Before becoming New Zealand's youngest Prime Minister in over 150 years, **Jacinda Ardern** was a Member of Parliament, known for her progressive policies but not yet tested in crises.

She was recognised for her strong communication skills and people-first leadership style.

However, she had not yet faced global-scale adversity that would challenge her leadership at its core.

While she was politically experienced, she hadn't yet become a defining figure of compassionate crisis leadership.

She was respected, but she had yet to embody the quiet resilience of the **Nurse Shark**.

2. When the BYOS Moment Came, Ardern was Ready

Ardern's true leadership moment came in March 2019, when New Zealand faced its worst terrorist attack in history in the form of the Christchurch Mosque shootings, which killed fifty-one people.

The country was in shock and grief, and the world watched how its leader would respond. Instead of reacting with anger or divisive rhetoric, Ardern chose empathy, unity, and quiet strength.

She wore a headscarf in solidarity, embraced victims' families, and led a swift yet compassionate response by enacting strict gun reforms within weeks.

The Turning Point: Instead of responding with aggression, which would have been accepted by the people (given the circumstances), she opted to lead through calm strength, compassion, and decisive action.

3. Ardern Delivered, and How!

Ardern's approach to leadership was tested again during the COVID-19 pandemic, where she faced immense pressure:

✓ Implemented one of the world's strictest early lockdowns, prioritising public safety over political convenience.

✓ Delivered clear, reassuring communication, reducing fear and misinformation.

✓ Used empathy instead of force, reinforcing New Zealand's "team of five million" mindset, encouraging collective responsibility.

✓ Kept the death rate among the lowest globally, proving that calm, measured decisions could save lives.

Instead of acting out of fear or panic, Ardern used **Nurse Shark** leadership by remaining calm, steady, and strategic.

4. Her Actions Spoke Aloud

✓ Ardern became a global symbol of empathetic leadership in times of crisis.

- ✓ She earned worldwide praise for her human-first approach to governance.
- ✓ Showed that leadership isn't about dominance, but about trust, transparency, and quiet resilience.
- ✓ Inspired a new model of political leadership, proving that compassion and decisiveness can coexist.

Jacinda Ardern's leadership proved that power need not always be loud or aggressive.

Sometimes, the strongest leaders are the ones who move with patience, empathy, and quiet strength.

Go for It!

"In stillness, find strength. In persistence, find growth. Find your Deep Waters."

From Stillness to Power

Resilience and quiet strength give you the foundation to endure challenges. But when the moment calls for bold action, stillness must give way to power.

In the last shark chapter ahead, we bring to you the **Great White Shark**, the most iconic of the species.

The **Great White Shark** doesn't hesitate. It commands with authority, leads strategically, and takes control by relying on its instincts and expertise.

Now, it's time to acquaint yourself with this style of leadership.

Chapter 9: The Great White Shark – Power, Leadership & Fearlessness

Meet the Great White Shark

Scientific Name: *Carcharodon carcharias*

Habitat: Coastal and offshore waters worldwide.

Behaviour: Powerful apex predators, exuding authority and control.

Unique Trait: Known for their dominance and fearless presence.

Commanding respect, the Great White Shark leads by exuding power and fearlessness.

Story: "Ethan's Apex Moment"

1. A Veteran in Corporate Security

In the high-rise secure operations centre of **TriAxis Ventures** overlooking London's Canary Wharf, Ethan Taylor, the Head of Corporate Security, monitored incoming threat alerts. His role was critical: safeguarding the company's vast network of data centres across Europe.

As a former Marine Corps officer, Ethan was no stranger to pressure. The room buzzed with tension as a routine cyber threat simulation tested his team's response times.

"This is a battlefield," Ethan thought, his sharp eyes scanning the dashboard.

2. A Crisis Unfolds

The simulation ended abruptly when a real alert flashed on the screen. TriAxis's Frankfurt data centre, the largest in its network, was under a ransomware attack. Losing these servers would mean catastrophic financial and reputational damage.

"This is no drill," Ethan barked, rallying his team. The room erupted into controlled chaos.

Satya, the CTO, who had been overseeing the simulation, approached Ethan. "This is massive, Ethan. Can you handle it?"

Ethan nodded. Leadership, he knew, wasn't about avoiding pressure but confronting it decisively.

3. Enter the Great White Shark

As he moved to the strategy room, Ethan steadied himself as he studied a wall of data streams showing the attackers' movements.

Kandahar. Dust. Decisions that meant life and death. As a Major, Ethan had learnt how to thrive under pressure, whether coordinating evacuations under fire or managing limited resources in hostile territory.

This wasn't a war situation, but the stakes were high. "This isn't Kandahar," he reminded himself, "but fearless leadership still applies."

His team looked to him for answers, their faces mirroring the doubt and fear he had seen before in Kandahar. Frankfurt's servers were under relentless attack, and every passing minute increased the risk of catastrophic data loss.

The Great White Shark doesn't attack recklessly. It calculates, waiting for the perfect moment to strike with full force.

Ethan realised that leadership wasn't about constant aggression. It was about acting with fearless precision.

He raised his voice, steady but commanding, cutting through the noise.

"We don't have time to overthink this. Here's the plan: isolate the servers, contain the breach, and back up priority systems. No deviation, no hesitation."

He assigned roles to his team with precision, dividing them into three groups:

- ✓ Triage units to contain the attack
- ✓ Analysts to decrypt the ransomware
- ✓ A liaison officer to coordinate with Interpol's Cybersecurity Task Force.

The first reports started rolling in. The hackers had escalated their attack, targeting backup systems by deploying a worm to spread across the network faster than anticipated.

Ethan adjusted his strategy. "Redirect resources to stabilise the core systems and block external access to Frankfurt," he commanded. His calm yet authoritative tone steadied the team.

True power emerged as courage met clarity.

4. The Suspense Heightens

As the attackers breached the backup protocols, a critical decision loomed. Deploying the encryption patch would take twelve minutes, but the attackers could corrupt the secondary storage in ten.

Ethan's voice cut through the tension. "Activate the decoy servers and reroute the attack. Give them a target."

The team hesitated but followed his lead. As the decoy servers bore the brunt of the attack, the encryption patch was deployed successfully. Finally, the red alerts disappeared, and the Frankfurt servers stabilised.

A collective exhale swept the room. Ethan allowed himself a small smile. It signified relief, mixed with the weight of responsibility.

5. The Turning Point

Satya entered the room as the Frankfurt servers stabilised.

"You didn't flinch, Ethan. Not even when it felt impossible."

Ethan nodded, smiling despite the fatigue etched into his face. "I was scared, Satya. But I decided not to avoid fear, but use it as a fuel to make decisive, fearless choices and guide others through it."

Later, Satya praised Ethan's composure and offered him a global leadership role. "The team's started calling you the **Great White Shark**," he added with a grin. "Calm above the surface, relentless beneath it."

As Ethan stood on the Thames' edge that evening, he reflected not just on the crisis he had resolved, but on what it meant to stand at the helm in turbulent waters. He wasn't expected to know every answer. It was more about exuding certainty, creating clarity, and inspiring confidence when none existed.

The Great White Shark doesn't hesitate, and neither would he.

He also figured out another interesting aspect. His ability to claim responsibility in the midst of chaos had reflected the bold ownership of the Blacktip Shark, which laid the foundation for his fearless leadership as the Great White Shark.

Great White Shark Insight: Apex Zone

- ✓ To lead is to embody the presence of the Great White Shark: bold, decisive, and unwavering.
- ✓ Lead where it matters most.

How often do you hesitate when the tide rises? How many opportunities are lost because fear paralyses action?

If you've ever been in a situation where leadership beckoned but fear held you back, what stopped you? What would you do differently now?

Think about the challenges you face today where bold decisions and decisive action are needed. What steps can you take to prepare yourself to be the leader your team needs in those moments?

Great White Shark Exercise: Step into a Leadership Opportunity

Do This Today: Identify a meeting or situation where you feel you can lead your team decisively. Prepare a clear plan and take the lead.

Do This Later: Reflect on how taking decisive action influenced the team's trust and the outcome.

Real-World Example: Indra Nooyi's Bold Leadership through Fearless Execution

1. Paving the Way, Owning her Destiny

Before **Indra Nooyi** became one of the most powerful CEOs in the world, she was an ambitious strategist rising through the corporate ranks.

She had played key roles in PepsiCo's strategic planning, helping steer acquisitions.

However, PepsiCo's business model was deeply rooted in sugary sodas and processed snacks, making it a short-term profit machine rather than a long-term sustainability leader.

Nooyi was highly respected within the company, but she hadn't yet stepped into the full fearless leadership mode of the **Great White Shark**.

She was a rising force, but not yet the bold visionary who would redefine PepsiCo's future.

2. Breaking down Barriers

In **2006**, when Indra Nooyi became CEO of PepsiCo, she faced critical crossroads:

- ✓ Investors wanted to double down on soda and junk food sales, which were still highly profitable.
- ✓ Health-conscious consumers were shifting their preferences, demanding healthier alternatives.
- ✓ The food industry was resistant to change, unwilling to sacrifice short-term profits for long-term sustainability.

Instead of playing it safe, Nooyi chose the **Great White Shark** mindset of dominating the deep waters by making fearless, industry-defining decisions.

3. Indra Nooyi's Bold Leadership: Creating New Benchmarks

Rather than following the easy path of maximising short-term gains, Nooyi:

✓ Pushed PepsiCo toward a healthier future, rebranding it as a company that cared about wellness and sustainability.

✓ Reformulated products, reducing sugar, salt, and unhealthy ingredients despite criticism from traditionalists.

✓ Acquired brands like Tropicana, Naked Juice, and Quaker Oats, expanding PepsiCo beyond soda.

✓ Set long-term environmental and ethical goals, pioneering sustainability in the food industry.

Her bold decisions were initially met with investor scepticism and internal resistance. Some feared she was weakening PepsiCo's core business, but Nooyi stood her ground, knowing that true leadership means making tough calls.

4. Outcomes of Nooyi's Visionary Leadership

✓ PepsiCo's revenue grew from $35 billion to over $63 billion under Nooyi's leadership.

✓ The Company became a sustainability leader, proving that ethical business practices and profit can coexist.

✓ She was named one of the most powerful women in business, inspiring a new generation of leaders.

- ✓ She proved that fearless decision-making is not about being reckless, but about having the courage to challenge norms and drive change.

Indra Nooyi showed that true leadership means standing firm in the face of resistance, making bold moves, and commanding respect. And that amounts to not just being powerful, but being visionary.

It's Your Turn Now!

"Fear is the raw material from which courage is forged. Be the Great White Shark. Fearless, powerful, and in control."

So, What's Next?

Is responding to challenges the only way to grow? Perhaps leadership isn't just about displaying courage, agility, persistence or fearlessness, but also nurturing empathy and trust.

In a few places earlier in the book, I had hinted at something other than shark behaviour, like the right environment, trust and connections.

Well, the wait is over. Turn the page to uncover the surprise...

Part 4: The Hidden Card

Sometimes, what you need isn't a shark circling your tank, but a dolphin swimming beside you.

Why Dolphin?

In the world of relentless pursuits and constant deadlines, we often celebrate aggression, speed, and dominance, which are the traits of sharks.

But what happens when the problem isn't external, but deeply internal? When it's not about chasing prey, but about staying afloat?

Not every situation needs a shark. Sometimes, what we truly need is a dolphin, because:

- They don't dominate; they guide.
- They don't push; they lift.
- When we are vulnerable, bruised, and too tired to fight, they provide warmth, patience, and empathy.

A shark might push some of us harder than we need. A shark would say, "Just swim faster. Just survive." But many of us, at certain points in life, don't need survival tactics; instead, we need someone to remind us how to breathe.

True success balances decisive action with meaningful connections, creating a foundation of trust and collaboration. The dolphin teaches you the ultimate leadership trait: *empathy*.

Are you ready to create a lasting impact through trust and emotional intelligence?

Do You Need a Dolphin?

Sometimes, challenges at work or in life don't require more speed, aggression, or adaptability. They require empathy, patience, and emotional intelligence. Dolphins are not about fighting harder; they are about connecting deeper.

The Dolphin Quiz

Find out whether you need a dolphin or not.

Answer the questions below:

1. **You've been feeling emotionally drained** at work lately. How do you respond?

a) **Push harder** and suppress your feelings.

b) **Take a break** but feel guilty about it.

c) **Pause, reflect, and ask** for support if needed.

2. **You notice a teammate struggling** with personal issues, and it's affecting their performance. What do you do?

a) **Ignore it**, as it's their personal problem.

b) **Offer help** but feel unsure how to follow through.

c) **Sit down with them**, listen, and offer support without judgment.

3. **A major project hits an unexpected roadblock**. How do you react?

a) **Push the team harder** to meet deadlines.

b) **Take control** of every detail yourself.

c) **Encourage the team** to regroup, share concerns, and find a collective way forward.

4. **In meetings**, do you feel that **your voice, or others', is often unheard**?

a) **I push louder** to be heard.

b) **I stop speaking up** altogether.

c) **I calmly create space** for everyone, including myself, to share thoughts.

5. When was **the last time you celebrated** a team or personal win?

a) Wins are **just another task** crossed off the list.

b) I noticed, but **we didn't really celebrate.**

c) I made sure that **we paused, reflected, and appreciated** the effort.

Scoring:

- **Mostly A's**: You're leaning heavily on force and resilience, but you might be ignoring emotional connections. A dolphin could bring the balance you need.
- **Mostly B's**: You're aware of the need for connection and empathy, but struggle to act on it consistently. A Dolphin's guidance could help you unlock this.
- **Mostly C's**: You already embrace a dolphin's mindset. Empathy, patience, and trust are your strengths. Still, this chapter might refine your approach.

Chapter 10: The Dolphin – Empathy, Trust & the Power of Connection

Meet the Dolphin

Scientific Name: *Delphinidae*

Habitat: Oceans and coastal regions worldwide.

Behaviour: Intelligent, social, and deeply empathetic creatures.

Unique Trait: Known for their strong emotional connections and cooperative behaviour.

The dolphin thrives through trust, empathy, and collaboration.

Story: "Aarini's Ripple Effect"

1. A Child Misunderstood: The Making of a Teacher

Aarini was a fighter, even as a child.

At twelve, she wasn't like most of her classmates at **St. Raphael's School in Delhi**, one of the most prestigious institutions in the country. The school prided itself on high academic achievements, and Aarini... well, she didn't exactly fit the mould.

She wasn't a bad student. She was sharp, extremely sharp. She could grasp ideas quickly, but she wasn't the type to sit quietly and memorise pages of textbooks. She thrived in motion, whether on the cricket field, in hands-on activities, or in music. But in a school that measured success by grades alone, her talents often went unnoticed. Teachers had the following feedback to give:

- She has potential, but she's too distracted.
- She's bright, but she needs to focus on her studies.
- Sports and music are fine, but that won't build a career.

Aarini heard these words again and again from her teachers, and they made her feel unseen, unheard. They measured her worth in grades but never in the fire that she carried within. No one tried to understand her. No one tried to connect. The only person who truly saw her was her father.

2. A Father's Gift: Pushing Her Toward Cricket

Aarini's father had been a sportsman, a former state-level sprinter, who never got the chance to compete nationally due to financial constraints. He saw in her a natural athleticism, a hunger for movement, a fire to push beyond limits.

He refused to let her talent go to waste.

While Aarini's teachers saw her as a problem to be fixed, her father saw her for who she truly was. He connected with her, not by forcing discipline as her teachers had done, but by understanding what she needed. He knew that trust builds champions, not pressure. So instead of demanding results, he stood beside her, shaping her journey, one morning at a time.

- He woke up at 5:00 AM to take her to cricket training.
- He made her do drills in the park, emphasising footwork, strength, and endurance.
- He stayed at the nets for hours, giving her real-time feedback on her shots.
- When she felt like giving up, he reminded her: "Champions aren't made in comfort, are they?"

His discipline shaped her game, her mindset, her resilience.

And it worked. By fifteen, she was the captain of her school team. By eighteen, she was playing state-level tournaments.

Her father's guidance had changed her life.

But what if she had also been pushed further in music?

3. The Accidental Musician

Music was never meant to be part of her story. It happened by accident one afternoon, while she was serving detention for missing an assignment. The punishment? Sitting in the music room while the school band practised.

She sat in the corner, bored, absentmindedly drumming her fingers on her desk.

The band's conductor, a strict but observant teacher, noticed.

"You keep time well," he remarked, handing her a pair of drumsticks.

Before she knew it, she was behind the percussion set, hesitantly tapping along. By the end of the session, she was in the school band.

She realised she had a natural rhythm. But unlike cricket, no one pushed her to pursue it seriously.

So, while she played at school functions and enjoyed it, music never became something she trained for, something she excelled at, something she was known for.

It faded into the background, remaining an untapped potential.

Years later, after her cricket career, she made an unconventional choice.

She became a teacher.

Maybe she was not meant to follow the system, but to change it from within.

4. A Classroom of Hidden Potential: Two Students, Two Journeys

Aarini walked into Grade 6, Section B of Saraswati Vidya Mandir, a modest but vibrant school in Jaipur.

She could sense the students who were struggling, not because they were slow, but because they were misunderstood. She knew what it was like to feel unseen in a world that didn't know how to nurture you.

Aarini did what no one had done for her; she listened, she connected, she built trust before expectations.

Two students, in particular, stood out.

a. Ayaan, the Fearful Speaker.

Ayaan knew the answers but never raised his hand. He avoided eye contact, dreading the moment when teachers would call on him in front of the class.

One day, after class, she asked him to stay back.

"Ayaan, do you like cricket?" she asked him.

He nodded cautiously.

"What's your favourite team?" she prodded him again.

"India," he said softly. "And Chennai Super Kings."

She smiled.

"Okay, let's try this. Tomorrow, we'll start the class differently. I'll ask you a question about cricket. You answer. No pressure."

The next day, she asked him a simple question about MS Dhoni. He answered immediately.

She clapped. The class clapped. And for the first time, Ayaan spoke without fear.

Over time, he gained confidence. Until one day, he raised his hand on his own.

b. Myra, the Musician No One Noticed

Myra was always humming tunes in class, making rhythms with her feet. Teachers saw this as a distraction, scolding her for "not paying attention."

Aarini saw something different. Myra wasn't distracted. She was searching for a rhythm no one had given her permission to find. She wasn't just tapping her feet; she was expressing something no one had taken the time to listen to. Aarini felt an ache in her chest. This was what had been missing in her own life; someone who didn't just see talent but also understood its need to be nurtured.

"Myra, do you like music?" she asked. Myra nodded cautiously.

"What instrument do you play?" To which, Myra replied, "...Nothing. I wanted to learn, but no one thought it was important."

That hit Aarini deep.

This girl was exactly like her younger self. Her teachers had overlooked her potential simply because it didn't fit the traditional structure.

That year, for the school's annual event, Aarini formed a student band and also made sure Myra was in it.

On the day of the performance, Aarini didn't just stand on the sidelines. She picked up the percussion sticks and played alongside them.

For the first time, Myra wasn't just another student. She was seen.

5. The Reunion: The Power of Trust Over Time

Years later, Aarini often wondered: "Did my small interventions really matter?"

Then, one day, she received an invitation to the school reunion for the alumni.

To her surprise, she saw two familiar faces waiting for her.

- Ayaan had become a lawyer, advocating for underprivileged women. His voice was now his greatest strength.
- Myra had become a music therapist, working with children to help them express themselves through music.

Dolphins thrive in pods, using trust and communication to navigate their challenges. Aarini realised that leadership wasn't about pushing harder; it was about working together.

Aarini had been their dolphin.

She hadn't just taught them. She had seen them, she had heard them, she had trusted them long before they learned to trust themselves. Just as her father once did for her.

And in that moment, she realised that the most powerful gift a teacher can give isn't knowledge, but connection.

6. The Dolphin Mentality: Driving Leadership Through Trust

How do dolphins develop trust?

- They teach by creating a safe environment.
- They understand unspoken struggles and nurture growth.
- They don't command respect. They earn respect through empathy.

Maybe the world doesn't just need more leaders. It needs more people who listen before they lead, who build trust before they demand results.

Maybe the world needs more dolphins.

7. How to Find and Embrace Your Dolphin

Dolphins are everywhere; in your workplace, your friend circle, and sometimes even strangers you meet briefly. But finding and embracing them requires vulnerability.

- Be open about your struggles. Dolphins cannot help if they don't know.

- Pay attention to small gestures. A cup of coffee, a handwritten note, a quiet conversation.
- Don't dismiss kindness. Small acts can have the biggest impact.
- Most importantly: Accept help. It's okay to lean on others. Tomorrow, it could be your turn to help.

Dolphin Insight: Echo of Wisdom

- ✓ Sometimes, you need to bring a dolphin along to create trust, patience, and quiet wisdom.
- ✓ Empathy unlocks what pressure can't.

Growth isn't always about force. It's often about listening, reflecting, and trusting the process.

Take a moment to think about your own dolphins:

- Who are the people in your life who have shown up quietly and patiently?
- What small gestures have helped you during your difficult moments?
- Are you being seen as a dolphin by someone else right now?

Dolphin Exercise: Learn Empathy and Support

Do This Whenever Possible: Identify one colleague or friend who seems overwhelmed by his current circumstances. Offer actionable help, such as assisting with a task or lending an empathetic ear.

Do This Once You Observe the Impact: Reflect on how your support affected the person and strengthened your connection.

Real-World Example: Princess Diana's Compassion That Transcended Boundaries

1. Love and Admiration, From a Distance

Before **Princess Diana** became an icon of compassion and humanitarianism, she was a member of the British royal family, expected to fulfil her duties within the traditional constraints of monarchy.

She was widely admired for her grace and elegance, but in the early years of her royal life, she was struggling to find her true voice.

The monarchy had long operated with a stoic, distant image, emphasising duty over emotion.

At this stage, Diana was loved for her beauty and title, but she hadn't yet become the global humanitarian force that would define her legacy.

She had the platform, but she hadn't yet fully embraced the power of deep emotional connection, which was the defining trait of the dolphin.

2. The Embrace of Empathy (The Dolphin Moment)

Diana's defining moment came in 1987, when she publicly shook hands with an AIDS patient in a London hospital.

At the time, HIV/AIDS was deeply misunderstood, and there was widespread fear that it could be transmitted by casual touch.

Even world leaders and public figures avoided physical contact with those suffering from the disease.

But Diana broke the stigma in a single moment by offering her hand, without gloves, to an AIDS patient, proving that compassion should never be withheld due to fear.

This simple, yet groundbreaking act showcased Diana's ability to build trust, dissolve fear, and offer emotional support through action, not just words.

3. From Connection to Compassion

Diana didn't stop at symbolic gestures. She embraced the dolphin's path fully, dedicating her life to humanitarian causes:

- ✓ Advocated for AIDS patients worldwide, showing the world that they deserved dignity and love, not fear.
- ✓ Led the campaign against landmines, walking through active minefields to highlight the dangers.
- ✓ Connected with marginalised communities, sitting with homeless people, comforting sick children, and listening deeply to the unheard.
- ✓ Redefined the role of a royal, shifting it from mere diplomacy to genuine, human-centred impact.

Her kindness wasn't passive; it was active, courageous, and deeply transformative.

4. The Impact of Empathy and Love

Princess Diana, through her ability to connect with empathy:

- ✓ Became one of the most beloved humanitarians in modern history.
- ✓ Changed global perspectives on AIDS, mental health, and war victims.
- ✓ Left a legacy that continues through her sons, Prince William and Prince Harry, in their charitable work.
- ✓ Proved that emotional intelligence is one of the most powerful forces for change.

Diana's greatest impact wasn't through politics or policy; it was through empathy, emotional intelligence, and her ability to break down barriers with love and connection.

A Call for You to Take!

"You don't always need a shark. Sometimes, you need a dolphin. And when you find one, let it swim alongside you."

Conclusion: The Ocean Awaits – What's Next?

Looking Back

The journey across the deep waters of this book has brought you face-to-face with a variety of sharks and, finally, the dolphin.

Each chapter was not just about a creature. It was *you* all the way. It was about recognising the moments when you froze, hesitated, adapted, endured, or needed support.

At the beginning of this book, we asked you to "Bring Your Own Shark." By now, you have seen how each shark served a specific purpose, whether it was speed, focus, persistence, or adaptability. And then came the dolphin, reminding us that sometimes, empathy, trust, and a listening ear are what we truly need.

While the shark keeps us sharp, the dolphin ensures we thrive collaboratively and sustainably. The balance between these two energies transforms growth from a temporary sprint to a long-lasting journey.

1. What It Means to Bring Your Own Shark

Each chapter brought you not just a shark, but also a reflection of yourself. And every shark you invited into your tank helped shape a version of you that's faster, sharper, braver, and more resilient.

Adopting a BYOS mindset means taking ownership of your growth by choosing the challenges that will inspire you, push you out of your comfort zone, and help you unlock your potential. It's about being deliberate and proactive in introducing the right level of discomfort to break free from stagnation.

Embracing shark traits is about intentional choice and adaptability, wherein you demonstrate the courage to face uncertainty and use it as a force for positive change.

2. It's All About Balance

Sometimes, growth isn't about adding more speed or strength. It's about finding the right balance between action and reflection, power and patience, and between sharks and dolphins.

At the same time, you need to channelise your inner dolphin and create a safe, trusting environment, both for yourself and for those around you. The shark and the dolphin aren't adversaries; they are complementary forces that create the perfect ecosystem for growth.

3. Why This Balance Matters

In leadership, work, and life, we constantly navigate between the demands of performance (shark) and the need for connection (dolphin).

While the shark drives focus, urgency, and action, the dolphin nurtures creativity, resilience, and collaboration. The balance of these energies empowers you to:

- **Adapt and Thrive**: Facing challenges head-on while staying open to support and new ideas.
- **Grow Sustainably**: Avoiding the burnout that comes from relying solely on external pressures.
- **Inspire Others**: Leading with both strength and compassion to build trust and loyalty.

Whether it's embracing a tough project, stepping out of our comfort zones, or redefining success, the shark symbolises the 'X' factor required to thrive. Paired with empathy and trust, this approach creates a balance that fuels both personal and collective success.

In the end, it's not just about surviving the tank but transforming it into a thriving ecosystem. Because growth isn't a gift we wait for; it's a choice we make.

4. Sharks and Dolphins Are Tools, Not Solutions

It's easy to walk away thinking, "I need to be a Great White" or "I need a Nurse Shark in my life right now."

But here's the truth:

- Sharks and dolphins aren't end goals. They are tools. There will be times when you need speed (Mako). Other times, focus (Hammerhead). And sometimes, a warm, reassuring presence (dolphin).
- The real mastery lies in knowing which shark you need, or whether you need a dolphin, at what time, and in what measure.

5. Why the Orange Fin?

The shark fin on the cover is **orange** for a reason, and now is the time to share it with you. It represents *your* shark, the one that isn't bound to any single archetype in this book. In reality, the shark you bring into your life is rarely pure Mako, pure Hammerhead, or pure Tiger. It is a unique blend of traits you need at this stage of your journey. Orange becomes the colour of that individuality, a reminder that your growth is not about imitating a shark, but about *creating* one that carries the precise combination of speed, focus, courage, manoeuvring, strength, empathy, or leadership required to overcome your challenges. Your shark is not blue, black, or grey. **It is yours.** And that's why it is orange.

6. Your Final Reflections

As you move forward, consider these questions:

- **What shark do you need to bring into your tank?** Identify the challenge or discomfort that will push you to grow.
- **How can you embody the dolphin for others?** Be the source of trust, safety, and connection that empowers your colleagues and loved ones.
- **Are you building a balanced ecosystem for growth?** Blend precision with compassion, immediacy with mindfulness, and bravery with understanding.

The key to thriving is not in choosing between being a shark or a dolphin but in knowing when to embrace each. Growth is not about avoiding challenges or relying solely on external pressures. It's about intentionally shaping the tank you live in.

The Sharks You Met, The Lessons You Carry

	Mako Shark	Move fast. Don't wait for perfection. Done is better than perfect.
	Hammerhead Shark	Stay focused. Broaden your perspective, but know your target.
	Bull Shark	Own it. Face conflict head-on with accountability.
	Blacktip Shark	Take charge. Own your space with clarity and presence.
	Whale Shark	Stay persistent. Trust the long game, even when results aren't immediate.
	Tiger Shark	Pivot boldly. When the moment shifts, change direction with confidence.
	Nurse Shark	Heal and rebuild. Know when to pause and recover.
	Zebra Shark	Manoeuvre smoothly. When the path narrows, adjust gently to move ahead.
	Great White Shark	Lead fearlessly. Leadership isn't about waiting; it's about showing up.
	And at times...	You don't need a shark. You need a Dolphin who understands.

The Power of Ownership

If there's one message you take away from this book, let it be this:

"Growth doesn't happen to you. Growth happens because of you."

You are the fish, and you are the one who decides which shark enters your tank. The power to grow, to challenge yourself, and to rise above inertia lies entirely in your hands.

It is not about waiting for the perfect moment or the perfect leader; it's about making a choice, right now.

Beyond the Pages

This book is not meant to end here. The lessons you have encountered are not confined to these pages. They are waiting for you to act on them.

- Take the quizzes again.
- Reflect on the prompts.
- Look around your tank - what shark is missing?

The real transformation begins when you apply these lessons in your world. Your workplace, your relationships, and your passions are all tanks waiting for the right shark.

The Ocean is Vast, So is Growth

The ocean is home to over 500 species of sharks, each with unique strengths that help them survive in different environments.

In this book, we've focused on select shark archetypes that offer powerful metaphors for growth. Some traits from other shark species naturally merge into the ones we've explored. For instance:

- ✓ **Lemon Shark (Curiosity & Lifelong Learning)**: The inquisitive nature of the Lemon Shark is reflected in the Zebra Shark's capacity to evolve and the Hammerhead Shark's dedication to focused mastery.
- ✓ **Goblin Shark (Innovation & Thinking Differently)**: Known for its unconventional style, the Goblin Shark's spirit is carried through the Tiger Shark's adaptability in unknown situations and the Hammerhead Shark's strategic clarity.
- ✓ **Basking Shark (Deep Observation & Slow Mastery)**: The calm, patient presence of the Basking Shark is echoed in the Whale Shark's perseverance and the Nurse Shark's quiet strength, where progress is steady, intentional, and deeply rooted in awareness.

Rather than isolating every trait into a separate shark, this book distils them into the most powerful and actionable lessons for enabling real-world growth. Eventually, evolution is about adaptation, just as these sharks have done, and just as you will on your own journey.

In reality, growth isn't about picking just one trait; it's about knowing when to embody each one.

A leader might need the unwavering persistence of a Whale Shark today, but the agility of a Tiger Shark tomorrow. A creative thinker might lean into the Hammerhead Shark's clarity, while also embracing the Zebra Shark's evolution over time.

The ocean doesn't force a shark to be just one thing. Neither should you.

The Online Quiz to Find Your Own Shark

The journey you have undertaken through the ten chapters has now evolved your thought process and understanding that growth needs to be claimed, not just pursued, and that sharks serve as a powerful metaphor for this growth.

It will therefore be interesting to revisit the Shark Quiz more deliberately. I urge you to take this final step to discover your deeper alignment with the attributes you need to bring into your "tank" by engaging with the sharks that best resonate with your journey.

For ease, scan the QR code below using your mobile device. You may want to save the link for later use or share it with others who might benefit from it.

We'd also love to hear your thoughts! Share your feedback and reviews on the web page—we value your insights.

Your Ocean, Your Rules

This is not goodbye; it is a handoff.

The journey does not end with identifying your shark; it begins there.

As you close this book, remember:

- You are the fish.
- The shark is your challenge. The dolphin is your support.

- You do not need anyone else to push you. Invite your own shark into your tank. Allow a dolphin to swim alongside you.
- The ocean is unpredictable, but so are you. Dive in. Swim strong. Lead boldly.

Closing Words

Growth is not about having all the answers. It is about asking the right questions.

Where is your tank stuck?

What is stopping you from taking the next step?

You already have everything you need. Now, it is time to act.

Do not wait for growth.

Bring it.

Acknowledgements

Every book is a journey, and this one wouldn't have taken shape without a few remarkable companions along the way.

First, to my friend and fellow soldier **Deepam Chatterjee**, an author in his own right, who showed me how to craft the perfect metaphor for this book. Your guidance helped me see beyond words and into the world of allegory—turning sharks into mentors, challenges into catalysts, and the ocean into a playground for growth.

Next comes my family, my personal ocean of strength and wisdom. **Harpreet**, my wife and my very own **Mako Shark**, whose unmatched speed and determination ensure that hesitation never stands in my way; **Akanksha**, my daughter, as persistent as the **Whale Shark**, steady and relentless in pursuit of what she believes in, reminding me that *'patience isn't just a virtue, it's a power'*. And **Rohan Bajaj**, the newest entry into my life—the **dolphin** I didn't know I needed, bringing balance, empathy, and a refreshing perspective on what truly matters.

Finally, to every challenge that has ever knocked on my door - a big thank you! You taught me that growth isn't something that the world hands to you on a silver platter. You have to dive into the unknown, find your own shark, and embrace the currents of change.

May this book inspire you, dear reader, to find your own shark. And, if you're lucky, you will spot a dolphin along the way.

With gratitude and a knowing smile,

Navinder Narang

About the Author

Navinder Narang is a distinguished veteran whose journey spans the Indian Armed Forces, the corporate world, and the world of ideas as an author.

He served with distinction in the Indian Army, taking on challenging assignments in counter-insurgency operations in the North East, counter-terrorism in Jammu & Kashmir, border security along the Punjab and Rajasthan frontiers, and amphibious operations in the Andaman & Nicobar Islands. His tenure also included guarding the Line of Control in high-stakes operational environments, where discipline, resilience, and strategic thinking were non-negotiable.

After taking premature retirement as a Lt. Col., Navinder Narang transitioned into corporate leadership, bringing the same rigour and commitment to excellence into the ICICI Group, where he has held senior leadership positions, driving operational excellence, facilities management, and sustainability initiatives at a national scale. His ability to bridge military precision with corporate adaptability has made him a respected mentor and strategic leader.